The COFFEE Book

The COFFEE Book

Dawn Campbell and Janet Smith

PELICAN PUBLISHING COMPANY
Gretna 1993

The word "Pelican" and the depiction of a pelican are trademarks of
Pelican Publishing Company, Inc., and are registered in the U.S. Patent
and Trademark Office.

Library of Congress Cataloging-in-Publication Data

Campbell, Dawn.
  The coffee book / Dawn Campbell and Janet Smith.
    p. cm.
  Includes index.
  ISBN 0-88289-950-3
  1. Coffee. 2. Cookery (Coffee) I. Smith, Janet (Janet L.)
II. Title.
TX415.C29 1993
641.6'373—dc20   92-45038
                                                           CIP

Illustrations by Dale Smith

Manufactured in the United States of America
Published by Pelican Publishing Company, Inc.
1101 Monroe Street, Gretna, Louisiana 70053

To coffee drinkers around the world

Contents

Preface

Many people, as they sip on a cup of coffee, are unaware of the intricate and varied history that has brought them this cherished ritual. Behind the coffee they are savoring is a long entertaining story of invention, migration, and unending effort to produce and extract the many flavors of coffee that continue to make it such a popular beverage. The extensive history surrounding coffee provides interesting anecdotes that even the most jaded collectors of arcane knowledge will appreciate. As coffee spread around the world, each country added its taste preference and its own way of brewing, resulting in a plethora of coffee drinks. Unique customs across cultures also added to the ritual of drinking coffee. We hope the recipes included in this book will open up a wealth of cultural coffee drinking experiences for our readers. Experiment and enjoy your journey to the coffee tables around the world.

Acknowledgments

The authors would like to thank all friends who have contributed information and their valuable time towards this book.

A special thanks goes to Dale Smith for his input and illustrations, David Burton for the initial typing, Karen Parrish-Hite for typing the manuscript with numerous revisions, Dale Hite for his expertise in design, William Grywinski for his expertise in liqueurs, and Linda Briscoe for the map lettering. We would also like to thank our friends and acquaintances from around the globe who have shared with us their knowledge of coffee making in their respective countries.

Also we wish to thank the following persons for their contributions: Karl (Austria and Germanic languages translations), Dawn's mom (Brazil), Bea (Canada), Enrique (El Salvador, Guatemala, Venezuela), Jurisdal (Indonesia), Orla (Ireland), Peggy (Italy and Romance languages translations), Sylvia (Nepal), Nunsy (Norway), Lenia (Peru), Betty (Philippines), Jessica (Taiwan), Tolo (Tanzania), Alaya (Tunisia).

The COFFEE Book

The Story of Coffee

Myth Meets Fact

The popular myth about coffee's discovery tells of an Ethiopian shepherd who discovered his goats frolicking in the pasture all night long with unnatural energy after they had consumed a strange fruit growing in the valley. The shepherd ate some of the fruit himself and was astounded by his physical and mental sense of well-being. Eureka! The humble bean contained in the fruit was on its way to fame and glory, with just a little bit of notoriety in passing. Eager to share his precious new discovery, the shepherd offered the fruit to a nearby monastery where the ingenious monks made a tasty, aromatic decoction from the berry. The monks made a wine of the fruit and it subsequently spread quickly through monastic orders, for the drink hastened mystical rapture and facilitated all-night chanting. News travelled quickly and soon the decoction prepared from the bean gained popularity in secular spheres.

Coffeehouses became very popular; however, they were at times deemed immoral because they were accused of drawing men away from their obligations to their homes and religion. The consumption of coffee was forbidden periodically. Each ban was relatively short-lived due to the strong appeal of this pleasurable drink. Despite early suppression on religious and political grounds, coffee became a universal drink in the Arab lands, eventually being considered the moral and sober alternative to the devil's advocates, wine and spirit drinks.

Kawah became a household word and was soon adopted into social customs as a featured beverage. Coffee was thrown at the feet of the bride at Arabic weddings as a religious offering. The Turks embraced the drink as well. It became a staple in the home, and failure to keep a steady supply of *Kavi* for one's wife was considered grounds for divorce.

Travellers from Europe returned with tales of the exotic beverage, and its reputation preceded its arrival in their homelands. Although *café* was regarded suspiciously by some Westerners as the devil's hellish brew, it became a Christian drink with the blessing of Pope Clement VIII, who savored the beverage.

Breaking the Monopoly

Coffee distribution was controlled by the Arabs, who for centuries held a tight and zealously protected monopoly on the cultivation of the coffee plant. Coffee's destiny, however, was not to be denied. In the seventeenth century, Dutch traders finally managed to steal some viable seeds and started commercial plantations in the East Indies (Indonesia). Inspired by the success of the Dutch plantations, a French officer under King Louis XIV reasoned that the plant should grow equally well in the French colonies of the West Indies. The officer, Gabriel Mathieu de Clieux, conspired with a gardener to steal a cutting from a coffee plant in King Louis XIV's botanical gardens. This he planted in a glass trunk; then he set sail for the West Indies. The journey was not an easy one for de Clieux and on more than one occasion he placed his life on the line for his precious cargo. Once, he fended off a Dutch spy who had managed to tear off one of the plant's limbs. Despite protest from the crew, de Clieux shared his meager ration of water with the plant when all the sailors were near to perishing of thirst. Finally, the ship arrived at the island of Martinique and this single plant gave rise to commercial coffee plantations that successfully rivalled those of the Dutch. Ironically, the initial cutting was taken from a coffee plant that was given to King Louis XIV as a gift from the Dutch.

Coffee established itself in French court circles under King Louis XIV, who had a passion for coffee and enjoyed preparing it for guests in his golden coffeepot. A few years later, after plantations started in Martinique, a dashing young Portuguese officer from Brazil won the heart of a French governor's wife in French Guiana. As a token of her love, she secretly pilfered some coffee cuttings to present to him. The cuttings, which he planted in neighboring Brazil, began what are now the largest coffee plantations in the world. Plantations sprung up in other parts of South and Central America and the Caribbean. The coffee beverage continued to spread and was enjoyed by more and more people around the world.

Across Cultural Borders

Today, coffee is the brew of choice for millions of people. It has provided us with a focus for innumerable social occasions, whether it be a cosy tête-à-tête between close friends or a gathering of many. Its rich wafting aroma transcends all political, ethnic, and class borders. In fact, think of how many people from all walks of life eagerly look forward to that first cup of coffee to perk them up for the day ahead!

Farmers in Tanzania cradle an earthenware mug of coffee in their hands before a long day in the fields; Colombian women prepare a pot of breakfast milk coffee for

A French governor's wife presented some pilfered coffee seeds to a dashing young Portuguese officer as a token of her love. Those seeds began the largest coffee plantations in the world, in Brazil.

their children; New York stockbrokers kick off their busy day with a shot of coffee; campers in the Rocky Mountains climb out of their cosy sleeping bags to embrace the early-morning sun with a mug of hot coffee; Italians slip into a cafe for a quick espresso before work. Even the tea-drinking nation of Japan now imports some of the best coffee in the world. One spa in Tokyo has replaced the traditional tea bath with a coffee bath (containing thirteen tons of soggy coffee grounds to soak in). Coffee—although we all drink it, each culture, it seems, drinks it just a little bit differently.

Coffee flavors differ as do methods of brewing. Coffee-drinking customs are also as varied as the cultures themselves. The drink can be served in cups or bowls of various sizes and shapes with a plethora of ingredients added as flavorings or garnishes. Our tradition of sharing and reflecting on the day's encounters over a cup of coffee exposes us to each country's time-honored coffee practices. It can be the occasion for humorous cross-cultural exchanges, many of them over just how we order that very cup of coffee. In England, when asked whether you want black or white coffee, initially you cannot help but wonder if there are white coffee beans, like white chocolate! One is often confronted with new customs that are at odds with our own cultural reference. In France, the serving of cafe au lait in a bowl instead of a cup may seem odd at first, although to the French it is a familiar tradition. Tanzanians, who hail from a country where coffee is presumptuously prepared for guests, and in only one way, are amused when they come into a European home and are first asked if they would like coffee, and then are given such a variety of options—cream or milk? strong or weak? sugar? one or two teaspoons? a little liqueur?

Some methods of preparation date back to A.D. 1000 while others are of more contemporary origin. A wide range of flavors can be discovered, from the bitter tang of espresso in Italy, or the more mellow flavors of Sumatran coffee, to the winey coffee tastes of Ethiopia. Foreign textures and sensations reach the palate when one sips on the very sweet and viscous Turkish coffee, where surprise awaits in the thick mud settling in the bottom of the oversized thimble cup. In America, the land of the bottomless cup, the mug is full of percolated coffee, from the moment the customers are seated to the moment they leave. In Rome, the coffee is spewed out rapidly and the small demitasse of fancy espresso can be finished in three gulps, while one is standing in a crowded bar. In Vietnam one can literally count the number of drops of coffee slowly dripping into the syrupy milk at the bottom of the glass and spend an equal amount of time drinking the lukewarm brew. The differences one finds when drinking coffee from around the globe are as varied as the cultural environments from which they have come.

The Rise of Coffeehouses

Coffee has entered our social consciousness in numerous and manifest ways. It is in our music, poetry, literature, and economics. In the eighteenth century, coffeehouses proliferated and were known to be centers for gossip and gambling, as well as places to embrace literary and political discussions. Coffeehouses became a threat to established social institutions such as religions; and, as these places gained more autonomy, they were periodically banned. Each coffeehouse had its own specific following of businessmen, literary types, artists, theater people, or musicians; a person would become known by the coffeehouse he or she frequented. Many notables such as Addison and Steele, Sheridan, and Goldsmith were the centers of coteries found in the coffeehouses of London. With the introduction of newspapers, intrepid reporters would routinely gather much of their news for the day at local coffeehouses. In fact, much knowledge could be soaked up at these establishments and thus coffeehouses around the great British universities were nicknamed "penny universities." There, students could supposedly obtain much knowledge for a pence—the price of a cup of coffee. The ubiquitous tip, a boon to waitresses and waiters, probably had its origins here. Patrons were expected to put a pence in a box inscribed with "To Insure Promptness" (T.I.P.).

Coffee is renowned for its stimulative properties; therefore, for much of its history it was believed to sharpen the mental faculties. Students pulling an all-nighter beside a coffeepot can certainly attest to this. William Harvey (1578-1657) bequeathed fifty pounds of coffee to the London College of Physicians as a tribute to the little bean which he deemed to be the source of happiness and wit. Whether the little bean actually increases our wit is another matter. An eighteenth-century anonymous wit challenged this assumption in verse:

> Coffee works a miracle
> for those of little wit.
> With every drop it sharpens the mind
> and doubles the memory.
> The most barren of authors
> is thereby made fertile.
> Every cup empowers us to gabble
> without pause,
> Spouting fable as history. . . .

Notable Coffee Drinkers

However, certainly some creative geniuses were coffee drinkers. Balzac, one of the greatest French novelists of the nineteenth century, drank liters of black coffee to aid and abet his marathon writing sprees. Voltaire, the French philosopher, is reputed to have drunk fifty cups of coffee a day, and despite his physicians' warnings of premature death, he continued this into his ninth decade. The more contemporary writers Jean-Paul Sartre and Ernest Hemingway did much of their writing in Parisian cafes. T. S. Eliot's mournful measuring of his life with coffee spoons brings the black brew into the realm of serious poetic contemplation in the "Love Song of J. Alfred Prufrock."

Women had minimal involvement with coffee during its early history. Fortunately, the movements to prohibit women from drinking coffee and the banning of them from coffee establishments have been overturned in modern times. Emma Goldman, the early-twentieth-century feminist and political activist, undoubtedly drank her share of the brew as she championed the rights of women and the downtrodden in her lengthy polemics. Most certainly too Gertrude Stein and Edith Sitwell served coffee at their numerous gatherings for artists and writers such as Hemingway, Picasso, Eliot, and Joyce.

Bach composed his famous "Coffee Cantata" in praise of coffee as well as to satirize a German movement prohibiting women from drinking coffee. Beethoven was reputed to obsessively count out sixty beans for every pot so he could enjoy a predictable cup of coffee. Contemporary poets and songsters such as Bob Dylan ("One More Cup of Coffee for the Road") and Mississippi John Hurt (in praise of Maxwell House) continue to eulogize coffee, not from the pulpit where it had once been denounced, but from the secular environment of the coffeehouse.

Coffee has endured as a creator of fact and fable, and a survivor of many prohibitions. In fact, coffee, it is delectably apparent, is still brewing after all these years.

Migration of Coffee

When we drink a cup of coffee, we continue the long and colorful history of the coffee bean. From its beginnings as a seemingly innocuous wild berry in Ethiopia, it has stimulated great interest and controversy. The innocent coffee bean has been praised and criticized, condemned as Satan's work, blessed by a pope, offered to saints, outlawed, and instituted. As a consequence of its incorporation into various religious ceremonies, particularly in Mideastern religions, coffee achieved a mythical status. In secular spheres, it has inspired inventive minds and facilitated communication as a social beverage. For this very reason, however, the widespread use of the little coffee bean fueled many a social conflict—so much so that it was the coffee itself that once became suspected as being a catalyst for subversive and immoral behavior. Despite controversy and the periodic prohibitions of its use, coffee has survived and continues to be an important element in social and commercial ventures. The following chronology reveals the many facets of coffee's intriguing history as it migrated around the world.

A.D. 600 The popular legend surrounding the discovery of coffee alleges that a shepherd noticed that his goats began frolicking around like young kids after munching on the red berries of the coffee plant, which grew wild in Ethiopia (Abyssinia). Eating some of these berries himself, the shepherd experienced the same stimulating effects, so he offered them to a nearby monastery as a gift. As Providence would have it, the monks discovered that, after drinking a decoction from these berries, they could stay up all night and pray, reaching exhilarating states of ecstasy.

In Ethiopia, coffee was originally rolled with fat into balls as a foodstuff to sustain nomads on their long journeys through the desert.

900 In Ethiopia, wine was made from the fermented pulp of the coffee berries. This beverage was called *Kawah,* meaning "spirit drink." The term *Kawah* was perhaps the origin of the word *coffee.*

1000 Coffee was prepared with boiling water and green beans. The beverage took on a mythical status and quickly spread through Arabia as an adjunct to the religious ceremonies of the Sufis. It was also prescribed by physicians for its curative powers.

1200   A decoction was made by roasting the beans and boiling them in water for 1/2 hour. Soon crushing the roasted beans became common practice in Arabia. With the crushing of the beans came the invention of a conical-shaped pot with a handle for boiling coffee grounds and water together (*jaswah*).

1400   Coffee plants are cultivated in Arabia near the Red Sea. The Arabs attempt to maintain a monopoly on growing the coffee plant in the centuries to come.

1470   Coffee reaches Mecca and the first coffeehouses spring up. The coffeehouses are soon criticized as centers for immoral beings and for turning people away from religion. The governor in Mecca forbids the sale and consumption of coffee and bans coffeehouses. However, due to public pressure, this ban is lifted.

1480   Coffee is drunk in Aden and Syria. Coffee is sold in the marketplace in a *petite* cup, the demitasse.

1550   Coffee is introduced to Persia.

1554   Traders bring coffee from Damascus in Syria to Constantinople in Turkey. The Turks embrace the drink with much enthusiasm. Coffee soon becomes popular and drinking coffee in public becomes a norm. It also becomes an integral part of domestic life, such that a marital law is instituted that a husband must keep his wife supplied with coffee or there are "grounds" for divorce.

1600   Around the turn of the century, the coffee drink is sold in Rome. Certain priests appeal to Pope Clement VIII to have coffee banned, claiming it is the devil's brew. He settles the growing opposition by trying a cup of coffee and, finding that he likes the taste, quickly baptizes it as a Christian drink.

1615   Venetian merchants were the first Westerners to import coffee from Constantinople.

1635   Oxford claims to be the first place in England where coffee is drunk.

1644   A French traveller named La Royne introduces coffee to France. Wine merchants object to the new drink because it affects the sales of their brew.

1650   A coffeehouse named Angel is opened in Oxford by a Lebanese called Jacob.

1652   A man named David Edwards, a merchant, brings coffee to London from Turkey. Pasqua Rosée serves coffee for sale to the public. Later, Rosée opens the first coffeehouse in London at Michael's Alley, Cornhill. With the opening of the coffeehouse, public coffee drinking in London begins, affecting England's social history dramatically.

1660   Coffeehouses in England become gathering places for the great minds of the time. Famous men like Addison and Steele discuss philosophy and literature and a wealth of ideas are exchanged.

Coffee customs continue to spread and develop throughout Europe, with each country adding its own sentiments and preferences to the ritual.

1663   Milk is added to coffee in Holland to reduce the bitter taste.

1665   In England, coffeehouses are well-established meeting places for men from all walks of life. Sober and stimulating conversations abound. Coffeehouses become a center for social life and gossip makes its rounds.

1666   After the Great Fire of London, coffeehouses are quickly rebuilt in the city. The custom of coffee drinking survives.

1669   Suleiman Aga, the ambassador of the Turkish government to France, popularized coffee drinking among the nobility.

1670   The Dutch introduce coffee to New Amsterdam (later New York). An early American settler, Dorothy Jones, of Boston, obtains a license for coffee peddling in America.

Coffee is planted in India by a Moslem pilgrim named Baba Budan.

1672   An Armenian street peddler named Pascal sets up a coffee tent at the Fair of Saint-Germain. He then opens up a coffee shop in Paris selling "Petit Noir" — meaning little cupfuls of coffee.

1673   Over 3,000 coffeehouses in London.

1674   In England, women were originally banned from coffeehouses. Men thought they had found a new freedom and a safe haven away from their womenfolk. In protest, women publish a petition in which they complain coffeehouses are tempting men away from their homes and responsibilities. The women also attest to "the fact" that coffee makes their men impotent.

1675   Charles II tries to close down coffeehouses. So great is the public outcry that shortly thereafter he relents. Coffeehouses will flourish during his reign.

1683   First Viennese coffeehouse, called The Blue Bottle, opened by a Polish immigrant, Franz Georg Kolschitsky. Milk and honey are added to filtered coffee.

1685   The French introduce the word *cafetière* (coffee maker).

1687   Invention of the coffee mill in France leads to the widespread use of coffee.

The Dutch manage to steal coffee seeds from Arabia, finally breaking the Arab monopoly on producing coffee. They successfully start growing coffee in the Dutch colony of Java. The word "java" becomes a slang term for coffee.

Custom of coffee drinking after a meal is firmly established in France (the "after-dinner" coffee).

1688   Edward Lloyd opens a coffeehouse in the Royal Exchange Building in London. Shortly after, Lloyd begins the world-famous Lloyd's of London insurance company. Much business is done in coffeehouses because so many business contacts can be made among the patrons.

Dealings in stocks and shares take place in numerous coffeehouses. Jonathan's coffeehouse becomes the center of these dealings and the first real stock exchange. Today the attendants are still called "waiters."

1689   François Procope, a street peddler, opens an elegant cafe in Paris. It is called Café de Procope.

1690   Coffeehouses open in America.

Coffee drinking eventually declines in England, largely because tea could be made easier by simply adding boiling water.

In the late 1600s, many Europeans drank coffee from small bowls made of pewter, silver, brass, or porcelain. It was quite common to drink coffee out of a saucer, instead of cups or bowls. Around this time handles began appearing on cups.

1706   A Java-born coffee plant is taken to the Netherlands for botanical display.

1711   The French begin to steep their coffee using a cloth bag.

1714   King Louis XIV is presented with a coffee plant from Dutch traders. The beans and successive offspring from these beans are disseminated throughout the French empire.

1718   Cultivation of coffee in Dutch Guiana (Surinam).

1723   French army officer Gabriel Mathieu de Clieux, under King Louis XIV, manages to pilfer a coffee plant from the Botanical Gardens in Paris, which he nurses and protects on a long journey to the West Indies. He succeeds in planting it in Martinique, initiating coffee planting in the West Indies (Caribbean).

The French colony of Bourbon, now the Island of Réunion, provides an important place for cultivating coffee, so important that the colonial government issues two decrees. One requires that every plantation grow 200 coffee trees. The second decree issues the death penalty for anyone who destroys a coffee tree.

1727   Francisco de Melo Palheti, a Portuguese officer from Brazil, wins the heart of the governor's wife in French Guiana. She presents him with some coffee plant cuttings as a token of her affections. The cuttings he plants in Brazil herald the beginning of what will become the world's largest coffee-growing plantations.

1730   Coffee is planted in Jamaica.

1735   Coffee plants growing in Santo Domingo (now the Dominican Republic).

1737   The plant genus *Coffea* is named by Paris botanist Antoine de Jussieu.

1770   Germans use chicory as a coffee substitute.

1770s   Coffee develops as a commodity crop throughout the world.

1773   Boston Tea Party begins the demise of tea drinking in America. Colonists protest the tax put on tea by the English government by dressing up as Mohawk Indians and dumping tons of tea from an English cargo ship into the harbor. Coffee starts to become a staple in American homes, and a symbol of patriotism.

1777   In Prussia, Frederick the Great restricts the roasting of coffee beans to only a few chosen persons. Coffee spies sniff out offenders and thereby guard coffee as a drink for the aristocrats. Rumors spread that coffee causes sterility.

1793   A group of auctioneers and merchants began meeting at the Tontine Coffee House in New York. Their endeavors eventually create the New York Stock Exchange.

1800s   In Germany, a home coffee break, Kaffeeklatsch ("coffee gossip"), begins among the aristocratic women. This period of time is an inventive one for coffee makers. The archbishop of Paris, Jean Baptiste de Belloy, introduces the drip pot. Shortly after, the café filtre and Napoletano coffee makers are invented.

1827   The pumping percolator is invented in Paris by Jacques-Augustin Gandais.

1840   Robert Napier, a Scottish marine engineer, invents the vacuum coffee maker.

1848 A great national revolution has its beginnings in one coffeehouse, the Cafe Palvax in Pest (part of today's Budapest). Political activists who frequent this coffeehouse initiate their part in history as instigators of Hungarian independence (March 15—Hungarian Independence Day).

1860s At Maxwell House Hotel in Nashville, Tennessee, a blend of coffee is developed and served.

1860 In France, people in all the social classes have become accustomed to coffee drinking.

1865 Soldiers in America's Civil War make campfire coffee.

1869 Leaf rust disease (Hemileia vastatrix) appears on coffee plants in Ceylon (Sri Lanka), marking the decline of coffee growing and the beginning of tea cultivation there.

1878 First ground coffee sealed in tin cans by James Sanborn and Caleb Chase.

1887 In Brazil, the world's first coffee research center, Instituto Agronomico de Capinas, is opened. Brazil has more coffee plantations than any other country in the world.

1890s A dried coffee extract is developed in America.

1898 A coffee dispensing machine used to sell large quantities of coffee to public is stationed at Leicester Square, London. The vendor is prohibited from vending in the "Square" a week later.

1900s Even though coffee originated in Africa, it was late in arriving to Kenya. Fine Bourbon coffee was planted in Kenya and Tanganyika (formerly German East Africa) by German settlers. The plantations were situated on the well-known mountain slopes of Mount Kilimanjaro and Mount Meru. The Germans left the tops of these mountain areas to the Chagga tribe, who planted coffee too. As it turned out, the upper mountain areas provided the best coffee. Thus, the Chagga tribe is one of the most "well off" tribes in Africa.

1901 A Japanese chemist in America makes a soluble dried coffee.

1903 A caffeine-free coffee is developed in America. It is called Sanka from the French sans caféine—meaning without caffeine.

1905 Dr. Ludwig Roselius from Germany develops a method of removing the caffeine from coffee (so one could get to sleep at night).

1906   Instant coffee becomes available. It is condensed coffee that can be reconstituted by adding boiling water.

1908   In Dresden, Germany, Melita Bentz filters her coffee through a linen towel, which eventually leads to the invention of the Melitta coffee maker.

Hill Brothers Coffee Corporation uses vacuum method of packaging roasted and ground coffee in U.S.A.

Dr. Ludwig Roselius patents his process in the U.S.A. and manufactures decaffeinated coffee in New Jersey. The government expropriates his company later in World War I as "enemy property." He must reestablish his company after the war.

1914   Coffee is part of the supplies and staples of soldiers in the First World War.

1920   The French Melior coffeepot is marketed.

1921   U.S. Patent Office records over 800 coffee-brewing devices since 1790.

1930   General Foods Company promotes Sanka, a decaffeinated coffee, marketing it for wide distribution twenty-seven years after its creation.

1930s   When English soldiers return to their homeland after World War I, many prefer coffee to tea. They start a revival of coffee drinking in tea-totaling England.

1938   Nestle's introduces Nescafe, a spray-dried coffee, in Europe.

1940s   During World War II, employers noticed their employees would work longer and harder if they had a supply of coffee to drink during the day. This was the beginning of the coffee break, which we now schedule into our day.

Automatic coffee machines were invented after the war by Lloyd Rudd and K. C. Melikain, two American ex-servicemen.

1950s   Italian espresso machines gain widespread popularity in restaurants and coffee bars in Europe. The use of these coffee makers increases demand for finely ground coffee.

The first English espresso bar, called The Moka Bar, is opened in London. Its success leads to coffee bars spreading throughout Britain where cups of espresso and cappuccino can be purchased. The coffee bars become the new place for teenagers to "hang out" and socialize. They also offer the British and tourists a taste of the Continent.

1960   Germany begins marketing the Melitta drip coffee maker, and paper filters for making coffee become popular in Western countries. Coffeehouses presenting folk musicians become popular in North America.

1962   Coffee-producing and -consuming countries sign the first International Coffee Agreement (ICA), designed to encourage cooperation among coffee exporters and importers, ensure a fair price, and promote coffee consumption.

1970s   North Americans travel in Europe in great numbers and they expect more in a cup of coffee when they return.

1975   A frost in Brazil occurs that dramatically affects the worldwide coffee supply. Brazil is the largest producer and exporter of coffee, responsible for supplying one-third of the coffee consumed in the world.

1980s   Coffee bars with espresso machines and exotic kinds of coffee and coffee makers rapidly replace standard restaurants. Special coffee cups are specifically designed for coffee drinking while driving. Automatic vending machines are designed to use freshly ground coffee beans for each individual cup selected, although they still use dehydrated milk powder.

1990s   With the growing environmental concerns, many take-out coffeehouses provide their own refillable coffee cups for patrons, to decrease the use of styrofoam cups. Disposable unbleached paper filters and reusable "gold" filters are marketed for drip coffee makers.

2000   For the future . . . a Canadian researcher created an "edible" material to be used as a replacement for styrofoam. The potential of this material (made from wheat) is unlimited. Environmentally hazardous styrofoam becomes a thing of the past and coffee consumers . . . well, after they drink their hot coffee, they can choose to eat their cups. And who knows? Maybe coffee is soon served in coffee-flavored cups where one can drink a ginger coffee (from Yemen) and "chase" it with a Colombian coffee-flavored cup.

Arctic Ocean

North
America

Atlantic
Ocean

Hawaiian
Islands

Mexico

Haiti Dominican
Republic

Puerto Rico

Jamaica

Senegal

Guatemala
El Salvador
Nicaragua
Costa Rica

Panama

Venezuela

Colombia

Pacific Ocean

Ecuador

South
America

Peru

Brazil

Antarctica

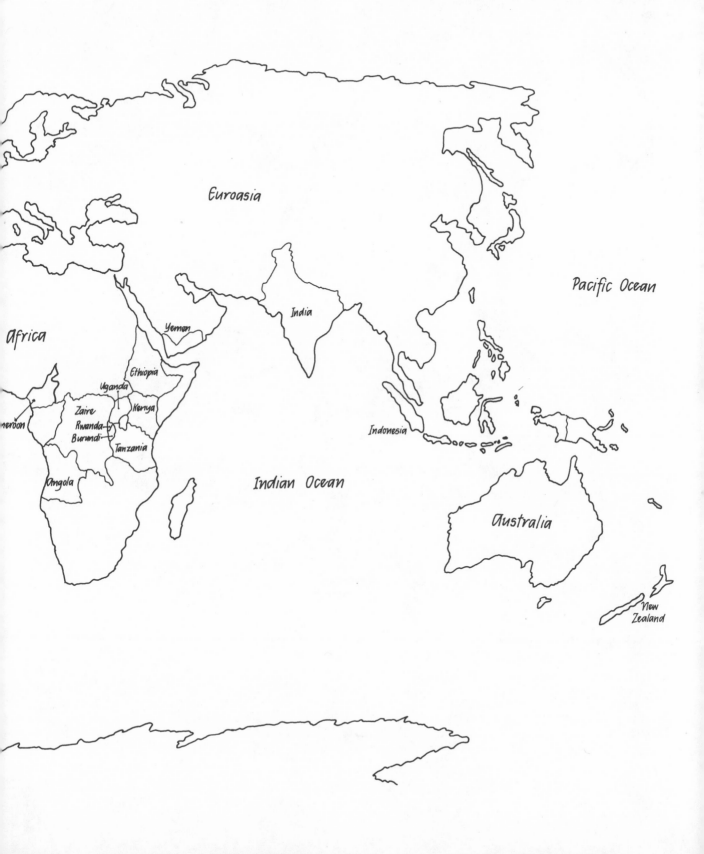

Euroasia

Pacific Ocean

Africa

Yemen

India

Ethiopia

Uganda

Zaire

Kenya

meroon

Rwanda

Burundi

Tanzania

Indonesia

Angola

Indian Ocean

Australia

New
Zealand

Coffee Beans Grown
in the World

The Coffee Plant

Coffee grows in subtropical and tropical areas at altitudes ranging from sea level to 6,000 feet. The coffee plant is an evergreen and if left unpruned will grow 20 feet high. There are many species of coffee growing wild; however, only two are grown commercially: *Coffea arabica* and *Coffea robusta (canephora)*. With the heavy rains, delicate white blossoms appear, which last for only a short time. About six months later, at the end of the rainy season, the tree's fruit, called cherries, emerge. The cherries swell and ripen from green to yellow to red. Inside the cherries, there are two coffee seeds (beans), which are surrounded by a juicy pulp and an outer skin.

HARVESTING

When the cherries ripen they turn dark red and are then ready to pick. In some areas with rainfall throughout the year, it is common to have flowers, immature berries, and ripe cherries on the same branch. Workers walk between the rows of trees, filling with ripe cherries the bags or baskets secured around their waists. An experienced picker can harvest about two hundred pounds of cherries daily. In areas with distinct seasons, cherries ripen at the same time and are left to dry on the tree. In this case it is much easier to strip the cherries from the branch with one brush of the hand. Mechanical means of harvesting are available in which the machine agitates the tree and then catches the cherries on a conveyor belt. This method is limited, however, because it requires a level terrain with long rows of trees. Coffee plantation workers are thus irreplaceable.

PROCESSING

Once the cherries are picked, processing removes the coffee beans from inside the cherries. There are two processing methods available: the wet (washed) method, used primarily for arabicas, and the dry (unwashed) method, used primarily for robustas.

In the wet method of processing, the cherries are first put through a pulping machine to break away the cherry's outer skin and remove most of the pulp. The cherries are then placed in large tanks of water to ferment for about twenty-four hours. Next, they are agitated and cleaned thoroughly with water. The beans dry in the sun for two or three days or can be machine-dried. Wet-processed coffees command higher prices because of the labor-intensive methods required.

In countries lacking sufficient water supplies, such as Ethiopia and Brazil, the oldest and simplest methods of processing are used. The ripe cherries partially dry on the tree and then are spread out in the sun for two or three weeks. They are raked and turned several times a day. Finally, the dried beans are put through a hulling machine to remove the dried pulp and skin. These coffee beans are referred to as ''naturals.''

SORTING

Sorting (separating) the coffee can be done by hand or machine. In the first method, workers pick out undesirable beans that move past on a conveyor belt. Machine methods include scanning beans with light or blasting with air to lift out lower-density (undesirable) beans. Typically beans are sorted according to size, shape, density, or color.

Species of Coffee

There are two major species of commercial coffee: *Coffea arabica* and *Coffea canephora (robusta)*. Arabica is a superior coffee with a rich flavor and excellent aroma. It is grown at a high altitude where there is good rainfall. Usually, the higher the altitude at which the coffee is grown, the better the quality. Arabica beans have one-half of the caffeine content of the robustas. Robusta is a hardier species of coffee plant, more disease and insect resistant. It was discovered at the end of the nineteenth century, flourishing at lower altitudes. The less expensive robustas are often used to add body to arabica blends. They are also used for many instant and commercial coffee blends.

Grades of Coffee

Coffee is graded according to the quality of the bean. The grading assesses the coffee beans' degree of firmness, flavor, aroma, and blending ability. Coffee-grading terms vary from country to country, so the reader is advised to become familiar with specific names. The following describes a general form of grading. Coffee beans are often blended to bring together the desired characteristics.

Supreme: the highest grade of coffee.

Prime Grade: the finest quality of bean grown at high altitudes. These can be brewed straight, yielding a flavorful, full-bodied brew.

Medium Grade: light-bodied, flavorful, slightly acidic, with pleasant aroma. These can be brewed alone although they are usually blended with other types to balance flavors.

Natural Unwashed: used as blenders to combine certain flavors.

Robustas: primarily grown in Africa. They have variable flavors and are used usually in blends to add more body or to tone down flavors. They also reduce the cost of coffee.

Coffee Tasting or "Cupping"

"Cupping" or tasting coffee is a precise and formal process in which a coffee is graded. Important decisions rest upon the taste buds of professional cuppers who rate the quality of a bean. Upon their verdict, coffee beans are exported, imported, used singly, or blended with specific other beans.

The Colombian economy depends on twelve *catadores* (professional cuppers) who decide which beans will be exported, ultimately continuing the country's reputation for producing many of the best coffees in the world. Cuppers must observe strict disciplines during their short career, which averages eight years, ending before the ripe old "cupping" age of thirty-six. To ensure a sensitive palate, they refrain from smoking, spicy foods, greasy foods, alcoholic beverages, and staying up late. Every six months, they go through a drink-grading test to guarantee objectivity.

On an average day, they taste about one hundred cups to ensure that the coffee being exported is not fermented, sour, poorly washed, or contaminated by molds. The green bean is first examined for appearance. Then it is roasted to the optimum color and then ground. Seven and one-half grams are precisely measured into a five-ounce cup. Boiled water, cooled slightly, is added and coffee infuses for a few minutes. When the lid is lifted, the aroma bursts forth, revealing any obvious defects and also what type of coffee is about to be tasted. As the grounds settle, the subtler flavors emerge — acidy, winey, floral, fruity, sweet, salty. Sweetness is detected on the tip of the tongue, acidity on the sides of the mouth, and bitterness at the back of the palate. With a single sip, inhaled noisily and swirled around the mouth, the cuppers can tell what region the coffee was grown in, the particular species, and the process used for gathering and preparation. They gauge each feature — acidity, body, and aroma — marking down their ratings. They also check for smoothness and balance of flavor.

There is a wide array of terms used to describe the characteristics of coffee. The following will give you an idea of both desirable and undesirable descriptors used to evaluate coffee:

Acidy (+): a pleasant sharpness of taste.

Baked (-): a flat taste, usually caused from under-roasting.

Body (+): the intensity of the sensation on the tongue. Full-bodied is a heavier sensation. Thin-bodied is a lightweight sensation.

Burnt (-): a smoky or charcoal taste, caused by over-roasting.

Fruity (+): a sweet aromatic flavor, similar to berries.

Green (-): underdeveloped fullness of flavor, mildly sour.

Musty (-): has moldy taste.

Rioy (-): harsh strong medicinal smell.

Sweet (+): smooth, absence of harsh or "off" tastes.

Winey (-): flavor resembling wine, usually caused by fermentation of beans.

With such an array of choices, one must rely on one's own taste buds, and experiment, to select a coffee for brewing at home.

Varieties and Flavors of Beans

AFRICA

In Africa, from the 1940s onward, robustas were planted because they are sturdier and more resistant to disease than the arabicas. The beans planted are thriving and, because of the smooth full-bodied liquor many yield, they are proving to be some of the best beans in the world for blending.

Angola

Robustas; grown in Ambriz, Andulo, and Gando regions. Yield pungently aromatic, heavy-flavored liquor; medium-sized beans, good in blends. Robustas from Ambriz district yield a neutral taste; used as bulkers/fillers in blends.

Burundi

Arabicas; grown in Ngozi region at altitudes of 4,000 feet plus. Graded AAA to BBB. High grades (AAA) yield rich, strong-flavored, highly acidic liquors. Low grades are very poor quality.

Cameroon

Arabicas grown in the northwest; yield sweet-flavored, mellow liquor. Graded by bean size: peaberries, standard size, elephant size.

Congo

Robustas; yield sharp-flavored liquor (tastes similar to Kenyan beans); used for instant coffees.

Ethiopia

Perhaps the home of the first coffee plants in the world, discovered around A.D. 600. The term *coffee* may have received its name from the town of Kaffa in Ethiopia, where coffee grows wild. Arabicas indigenous to this country are cultivated and grow wild. The main growing areas are Harar and Sidamo. Harar Mocha was the original mocha coffee bean. It has a distinctive aroma and flavor. Harar Mocha coffee beans yield winey-flavored, heavy-bodied, and highly acidic brew. These are the best of the Ethiopian coffee beans, the main coffee export of the nation. Graded by bean size: extra-sifted (large), longberry Harar (medium), shortberry Harar (small). Medium to high grown varieties grow around Agaro, Gimbi, Gore, Lekemti (in Djimmah region); the beans of this region produce pungently aromatic, winey-tasting liquors. Small beans are used for blending. In the southwest Sidamo region, small beans grow wild and are used for blending in dark roasts.

Ivory Coast

Robustas; yield pungently aromatic, heavy-bodied liquors; good added to dark roasts. The Ivory Coast is one of the largest producers of coffee in the world, next to Brazil and Colombia.

Kenya

Arabicas grown on the slopes of Mount Kilimanjaro and Mount Meru; yield mild-flavored (winey or fruit-flavored), delicately balanced, smooth-bodied, sharply acidic liquors; excellent in blends.

Liberia

There is a third species of the coffee plant (besides arabicas and robustas) called *Coffea liberica*. It is grown only in Liberia and used locally.

Malawi (formerly Nyasaland)

Arabicas; yield light, winey-flavored, full-bodied acidic liquor.

Rwanda

Arabicas from Cyangugu and Gisenye districts near Lake Kivu; yield rich, strong-flavored, good-bodied, highly acidic liquors.

Senegal

Robustas; yield an aromatic, pungent liquor.

Tanzania (formerly Tanganyika and Zanzibar)

Arabicas grown on Mount Kilimanjaro, Mount Meru, and Mount Oldeani. Those beans grown on Mount Kilimanjaro are sometimes referred to as Arusha and Moshi, named after the towns the coffee plants are grown near. Medium is grown in Southern Highlands, Mbeya, Mbozi, Rungwe, and Songea. Arabicas of high quality yield very aromatic, delicately acidic liquors. The best known coffee is Tanzanian Peaberry, used to blend with milder coffees. The arabicas from the Bukoba region yield a rich-flavored, mellow liquor with light acidity. Robustas, grown in Bukoba and Karagwe areas, yield neutral-tasting liquors. Highest grades are AA, A, and B.

Uganda

Produces Bugishu, an arabica coffee bean grown on Mount Elgon; yields winey-flavored, medium- to light-bodied, acidic liquor. Robustas are used in instant coffees and as bulkers/fillers.

Zaire (formerly Belgian Congo)

Arabicas grown high (4,000-7,000 feet) in Upper Zaire, Ituri, and Kivu districts; yield rich, strong, sharp-flavored liquors used in blends. Zaire produces robustas in the Kivu and Ituri regions, in the lowlands of Upper Zaire, and in the Equatorial Province-Uele district.

SOUTH AMERICA

Brazil

Arabicas are named for the states in which they are grown or the ports from where they are shipped: Bahia, Esperíto Santo, Goiás, Mato Grosso, Minas Gerais, Paraná, Paranaguá, Pernambuco, Rio de Janeiro, Santa Catarina, São Paulo, Vitória. Santos, the most well known coffee in the world, is grown around the São Paulo and Paraná regions and the southern part of Minas Gerais. *Santos* is the name for the size of the bean, not the area in which the beans are grown. Santos are used as the standard of coffee bean quality around the world. They yield a slightly nutty-flavored, smooth-bodied, slightly acidic liquor. The best quality Brazilian coffee bean is Bourbon Santos, which yields a sweet, subdued, acidic liquor. Maragogipe yields pungent, winey, acidic liquor; large beans. Maragogipe was a mutant coffee plant found in Bahia. It has been transplanted to Colombia, Guatemala, and Mexico. Rioy beans yield harsh-tasting, pungent liquors—not very appealing. In Brazil, sometimes a hint of allspice or cinnamon is added to the beans while roasting.

Colombia

Exports under the "MAM'S" label, which stands for Medellín, Armenia, and Manizales, the three major growing areas. The best coffee beans are found in the foothills of the Andes Mountains. Arabicas yield mild-flavored, full-bodied, medium-acidic liquors; considered to be some of the world's finest coffee beans. Maragogipe is the largest of Colombian beans; yields winey liquor with fine acidity; best in medium roasts (see Brazil above). Colombia standards for growing and grading coffee are very high. Even their medium grade coffee, Excelso, is of excellent quality; large flat beans. Supremo is the best grade coffee, characterized by bold, extralarge beans.

Ecuador

Arabicas grown in Cumbaya, Guayaquil, Manta regions; all are referred to as "Ecuadors." Yield sharp-flavored, medium-bodied liquors; used for blends. Generally of lower quality.

Peru

Arabicas grown in Cajamarca, Lambayeque, Piura, and San Martin regions; yield good-flavored, mildly acidic liquor. Chanchamayo is one of the better known coffees; yields aromatic liquor with good body and fine acidity.

Venezuela

Arabicas, from the regions of Caracas, Mérida, Táchira, and Trujilla, exported from port of Maracaibo. Beans exported from this port are called "Maracaibos." Caracas is the best known Venezuelan coffee and compares well with Brazilian Santos. Beans yield a mildly winey, light-bodied, acidic liquor. Mérida region beans yield delicate-flavored, highly acidic liquor.

CENTRAL AMERICA AND CARIBBEAN

Costa Rica

Arabicas; some of the world's finest coffees are low grown to medium grown in Costa Rica's central plateau regions—Alajuela, Cartago, Herediá, San Jose, and Tarrazu. Yield high quality, rich, sweet, sharply acidic liquor; large uniform-sized beans usually used in blends. Tarrazu and Alajuela beans, considered among the most aromatic in the world, are used for straight unblended coffee. Grading is also done by the hardness of the bean: Strictly Hard Bean (SHB), Good Hard Bean (GHB), Hard Bean (HB), Medium Hard Bean (MHB) for beans grown on the Pacific coast.

Cuba

Arabicas; yield mellow, slightly smokey-tasting liquor, with smokey aroma; good in medium roasts; flat beans used in dark roasts.

Dominican Republic

Arabicas, referred to as "Santo Domingos," grown in the regions of Baní, Barahona, Cibao, and Ocoa. The best yield slightly sweet, strong, full-bodied acidic liquor; large beans (the best are used for French roasts).

El Salvador

Arabicas are not graded according to region. Grades are Strictly High Grown (SHG), High Grown (HG), and Central Standard (CS). (SHG) and (HG) are the best and yield mild, slightly sweet, good-bodied liquors. Generally El Salvador coffees taste rather bland compared to those of some of their Latin American neighbors.

Guatemala

Arabicas; exceptional quality beans are from the regions of Antigua, Atillan, Cobán, Freihanes, and Huehuetenango. The best known are from Antigua and Cobán; yield sharp, strong, heavy-bodied liquors. Maragogipe beans yield aromatic, sweet, medium-bodied liquors; huge elephant-size beans; a favorite among connoisseurs, believed to be among the best Maragogipe beans in the world. These are the offspring of the Brazilian Maragogipe, a mutated arabica plant. The best arabicas yield smoky, rich-flavored, medium- to full-bodied liquor. Some beans are organically grown for export. Grades are Extra Hard Bean (High Grown) and Semi-Hard Bean (Medium Grown).

Haiti

Arabicas grown in the districts around Les Cayes, Gonaïves, Jérémie, Petit Goâve, Port-au-Prince. Gonaïves is the highest quality Haitian coffee bean; yields mildly sweet, mellow, good-bodied, light-to-medium acidic liquors; good in dark French roasts. The best grades are Strictly High Grown (washed) and High Grown (washed).

Jamaica

Arabicas, from the Blue Mountain region. "Blue Mountain" is a highly prized coffee with a delicate nutty flavor, full aroma, good balance of acidity; large beans, uniform size; best in medium roasts. This coffee is expensive and hard to come by. Not much of it is imported to North America or the Continent. Beware of coffees claiming to be Jamaican Blue Mountain. It is rare that you will actually be tasting the real thing.

Mexico

Arabicas from Chiapas (Tapachula), Coatpec, Córdoba, Jalapa, Oaxaca, and Hidalgo. Oaxaca yields nutty, sharp, good-bodied liquor; small beans; considered one of the best coffees in the world. Hidalgo and Jalapa coffees yield rich, good-bodied, acidic liquors. The best known Mexican coffee is high grown in the south central mountain region, near Coatapec. Mexican grades of coffee are based on growing altitude and the bean wash process: Strictly High Grown (SHG), High Grown (Altura), Prime Washed (Prima Lavada), and Good Washed (Bueno Lavado).

Nicaragua

Arabicas from Jinotega, Matagalpa, and Nuevo Segovia; yield aromatic, rich-flavored acidic liquor; large beans. Some bean organically grown for export.

U.S.A.

Hawaii

The only place in the U.S. where coffee is grown. Grown on the Island of Hawaii in the south central district of Kona on the slopes of Mauna Loa, in volcanic-lava-based soil. Beans yield rich, mellow, full-bodied, slightly acidic liquors.

Puerto Rico

Arabicas; yield rich, sweet, smooth, heavy-bodied liquors; large beans.

SOUTHEAST ASIA AND INDIA

India

Arabicas and robustas; usually grown on terraces in mountainous regions. Nilgiris from Tamil Nadu (formerly Madras) yields rich, strong, smooth, medium-bodied liquors with light acidity. Tellicherry and Malabar beans yield similar quality. The best known arabicas are Karnataka (formerly Mysore) and Malabar (Kerala State—formerly Travancore); high-grown beans; yield mild, sweet, heavy-bodied, low-acidic liquors. These beans used to be referred to as Mysores and Travancores. Monsoon Malabar is considered a unique-tasting coffee by connoisseurs.

Indonesia

Around 1878 many of Java's plantations were destroyed by the rust blight *Hemileia vastatrix,* the fungus that earlier destroyed the coffee plantations of Ceylon (Sri Lanka). After World War II, Indonesia replanted robustas, because of their sturdiness and resistance to disease. Low-quality robustas are grown in the Indonesian Archipelago on the islands of Bali, Flores, Java, Sulawesi (formerly Celebes), Sumatra, and Portuguese East Timor. The robustas from Indonesia are plain tasting and considered inferior beans, used only as bulkers/fillers.

Java: Arabicas; the best beans have pungent aroma, slightly spicy flavor, low acidity, and full body; make smooth roasts; small blue beans. It is rare to find true Java today as very little is produced. At one time Java coffee was so plentiful that coffee in England and on the Continent was referred to as "java," instead of "coffee." By world standards, only coffee from Java can be considered to be Java coffee. The beans are added to mocha to make mocha Java coffee (see mocha—Ethiopia, Yemen). The best mocha Java is an Indonesian-Yemen combination. "Old Java" (of which there are not many left) are green beans, which are matured for a period of up to three years before marketing. While the bean has a bit of an earthy taste and smell, it yields a slightly sweet, rich, smooth-bodied liquor.

Sulawesi (formerly Celebes): Arabicas; grown in Boengie, Kalosi, and Rantepao areas. Fine-quality beans yield aromatic, mellow, rich, heavy-bodied, acidic liquors.

Sumatra: Arabicas from Ankola and Mandheling regions. The highest quality beans are Mandheling; yield rich heavy-bodied liquors that are almost acid free. It is good in blends with highly acidic coffees; best in dark roasts. Considered by connoisseurs to be one of the finest coffees in the world. Some Sumatran coffee is deliberately held in storage for a year or more to develop a desirable smokey character. Aged coffee commands a premium price.

Malaysia

Arabicas and robustas; grown on small family plots and in Cameron Highlands for local use.

Papua New Guinea (formerly British Guinea)

Arabicas and robustas. Arabicas brought originally from Jamaica in the 1930s. The most common is New Guinea; arabicas yield rich, medium-bodied, well-balanced liquors; high grown. The New Guineans haven't developed their coffee market yet; however, the potential for producing a coffee sought after by connoisseurs worldwide is high. These are prize coffee beans similar in taste to the highest quality Colombians.

Yemen

Arabicas; grown at the tip of the Arabian peninsula. Mocha bean most likely named after the town called Mocha. Beans yield distinct winey flavor with bittersweet chocolate aftertaste; highly acidic liquors; small irregular-sized beans. Mocha by itself is too acidic, so it blends well with Java beans from Indonesia. By world standards, mocha Java coffee is supposed to have more mocha beans in it than Java beans. A popular blend around the world.

Roasts and Grinds

Roasting Coffee

The inherent aroma and flavor of coffee beans are brought out by roasting. This process involves heating the green coffee bean to different temperatures, which breaks down fats and carbohydrates into an aromatic oily substance. Sugars are caramelized with heat, resulting in darker colors and also more flavor and body in the coffee. The longer the bean is roasted, the less acidic it is, with slightly less caffeine content and a higher volume per weight.

TYPES OF ROASTS

Light or pale roast (light city roast): light cinnamon-brown color; preserves some of the delicate-flavor oils and is therefore used for mild beans. Preferred in England.

Medium roast (American roast): chestnut-brown color, a stronger flavor and mellower than light. Preferred in America.

Full roast (full city roast): rich dark brown color with a slight oil on the surface of the bean. The coffee has a strong flavor with a touch of bitterness. Preferred in Europe.

High roast (double or continental roast): shiny black beans with an oily surface; the coffee has a strong bittersweet aftertaste. Good for after-dinner coffees. Preferred by French and Viennese.

Italian roast (espresso roast): beans are black to the point of carbonization. Highest (longest) roasted, strong flavor. Preferred by Italians.

Roasted beans maintain their quality for only three weeks if stored at room temperature in an airtight container. Coffee may be stored for up to four months in a freezer.

Exotic Flavors

Flavoring can be added to coffee during roasting in the form of oils or powders. The warm beans absorb the flavor. Some retailers sell these powdered flavors separately to be added to the coffee grounds just before brewing. There is an endless number of these specialty coffees. More common ones are orange, hazelnut, chocolate almond, Irish cream, raspberry, and French vanilla.

Coffee Grinds

The roasted beans are ground before use so that they will release their flavors when exposed to water. Coffees can be used alone or blended with others before the beans are ground to yield balanced mixtures. Use the following grinds in the coffee makers specified, for best results.

Coarse Grind: open-pot method percolators
Medium Grind: plain infusion pots, plunger infusion pots, and percolators
Medium Fine Grind: drip pots with a metal filter
Fine Grind: steam-pressured pots (Vesuviana, Moka), espresso machines
Very Fine Grind: paper filter drip pots
Pulverized: Turkish coffeepots and Indian coffee powder

Once the coffee is ground it should be used within one week. Store in an airtight container to help preserve its freshness.

Instant Coffees

Several inventors experimented with instant coffee in the 1800s but it was not until 1930 that a coffee powder had any commercial success. The first step in making instant coffee involves brewing a very strong coffee mixture in a tall percolator. The liquid coffee concentrate is then dried using one of two methods: spray-drying or freeze-drying. In spray-drying, the concentrate is sprayed with very hot air from a high tower. Water evaporates, leaving powdered beads of coffee at the bottom. The beads are clustered into larger particles through a process of agglomeration. With freeze-drying, the liquid coffee concentrate is frozen and then placed in a vacuum chamber. The resulting dry granules can be ground into particles.

Decaffeinated Coffee

An increasing number of people are choosing to drink decaffeinated coffees. The Food and Drug Administration requires that decaffeinated coffee have 97 percent of the caffeine removed from the unroasted beans. The sales of decaffeinated coffee have gradually risen; today it captures 20 percent of the coffee consumer market. With an eye on the potential profits from sales of caffeine, companies have typically used inexpensive robusta beans, which have a relatively higher caffeine content than arabica beans. Fortunately, consumers have demanded better-quality coffee, so arabica beans are now being decaffeinated.

Decaffeination has been practiced since the turn of the century. All decaffeination processes start by steaming green, unroasted beans, to unbind caffeine from the bean. Then either the "direct" or "indirect" method is used to remove the caffeine.

In the "direct" method the beans come into direct contact with the decaffeinating agent. Steamed beans are drenched in methylene chloride solvent, which has an affinity for caffeine. The caffeine-laden solvent is drawn out and the caffeine is later removed. The beans are steamed again to remove any residual solvent and later roasting further evaporates almost all traces of solvent. Consumers tend to avoid the superior decaf of the direct method, because they are leery of chemical processes. Some think this fear is unwarranted because the minute traces of chemical remaining in the beans are equivalent to the amount found in city air.

In the "indirect" method, commonly called the water-process method, a water solution not only draws out the caffeine but also the flavoring compounds. This caffeine-water mixture is drawn off and treated with methylene chloride, which absorbs the caffeine. Heat evaporates the solvent and caffeine from the water. The water is reunited with the beans to allow them to reabsorb the flavorful compounds. Unfortunately, the low amount of solids and flavorings recaptured results in coffee that is only a shadow of its former self. A Swiss method has improved the water process method somewhat by using carbon filters rather than chemicals, which keeps more solids intact in the bean.

A new and promising process, first patented in 1970 in Germany, uses "supercritical" carbon dioxide. Green beans are softened with steam and then exposed to "supercritical" carbon dioxide—carbon dioxide at a high pressure and temperature. The carbon dioxide penetrates the beans to extract only the caffeine and it is then drawn off, leaving no chemical residue.

A Turkish ibrik.

Brewing Methods and Pots

Despite the variety of coffee makers available, there are two ways of extracting the flavorful alkaloids from the coffee bean, either boiling (using boiling water) or infusion (using water just below boiling point).

A plethora of coffee makers and gadgets have been invented solely for the purpose of transforming the coffee bean into a consumable beverage. This product is not made for our sustenance but rather for pure enjoyment. The coffee bean has spurred the creative imagination to perfect the coffee brew to match the expectations elicited by its tantalizing aroma.

Boiling Methods

TURKISH COFFEE METHOD

"Turkish Coffee" is made with one of the oldest surviving boiling methods, which became popularized in Middle Eastern countries under the names of "Arabic," "Greek," "Turkish," and "Armenian." The coffee boiler was actually invented in Cairo and later spread to Turkey. The coffee is prepared in a tall long-handled copper or brass pot, conical in shape. It is called an *ibrik* (Turkey), *briki* (Greece), *tanaka* (Egypt), and *rakwi* (Arabia). The coffee boilers come in various sizes making one to six servings and have a lip for pouring. Larger quantities cannot be made because the coffee settling to the bottom of the cup loses the necessary consistency and a good froth is not forthcoming. Guests are always asked what their preference for sugar is because sugar is added before the coffee during preparation. The occasion may also dictate the amount of sugar added regardless of people's preference. Joyous events such as weddings and birthdays call for the coffee to be very sweet whereas during sad events such as funerals, respectfully, the coffee should be bitter.

Method: Fill the ibrik half-full with cold water and add sugar as desired. Place on a flame and bring to a boil. Remove from the heat, add pulverized coffee, stir, and place over the flame. As soon as the coffee foams up to the rim, remove from the heat. Return to the heat and allow coffee to rise one or two more times. The coffee is poured into demitasse cups. A thin head of brown foam should completely cover the surface to be authentic. The foam has been referred to as the "face of the coffee" or the coffee cream. If the host serves coffee without it, he loses face to the guests. It is difficult to produce a good foam. People must practice the art in order not to disgrace themselves or insult their guests even though it adds no particular flavor. Middle Eastern countries enjoy a brew seasoned with various spices such as cardamom, cinnamon, cloves, and ginger.

It is common in many countries to prophesize people's fate from the grounds left in the coffee cup. After drinking the coffee, the cup is inverted, allowing the coffee sediment to drip downwards and create unique patterns on the side. An experienced fortune-teller can foresee a clear picture of your fate. Hopefully the grounds will be arranged such that one will have good health, prosperity, and happiness.

OPEN-POT METHOD

This method has continued to find supporters in many countries, despite claims that it is the worst possible way of making coffee. It is, however, one of the simplest methods. Some people boil the coffee for hours, while others bring the brew to a boil just briefly. Numerous techniques were employed to help settle the grounds, such as adding eggshells, egg white, or cold water. Legend has it that, for a dramatic effect, cowboys will hold onto the handle of the open pot and swing it up and around and down in a circle at their side to help settle the grounds. In the West of America, the coffeepot is never washed, so as to retain the collected essence of every previous pot of coffee. However, it should be noted that a seasoned coffeepot does not enhance the flavor; rather, it detracts from it. A residue of coffee oils that go rancid is unpleasant in any pot.

Method: Add water and coarse grounds to a saucepan. Bring to a boil for a few minutes and then turn the heat to low and stir well. Simmer for 20 minutes. Remove from the heat. Add a bit of cold water to settle grounds. Pour through a strainer into a coffee cup, or in keeping with the cowboy tradition one can even strain it through a sock. The coffee is often a bit murky due to the agitation of the grounds by boiling.

Infusion Methods

Until the eighteenth century, boiling coffee was the chief method of preparing coffee. In the eighteenth century, which was a particularly progressive period for coffee makers, numerous infusion methods were invented in which the coffee flavor is extracted from the grounds with water below the boiling point.

These methods produced a better brew by most standards. Boiling tends to damage the flavor. Initially, the better coffee essences vaporize, leaving the more bitter essences to be extracted into the brew.

STEEPING

The simplest infusion method is to steep the coffee grounds in water, strain or settle the grounds, and serve.

Hot Water Method: Bring cold water to a boil and allow it to cool for a couple of minutes in a saucepan or coffeepot. Add coffee grounds (medium drip grind), stir well, and cover the pot. Let the mixture steep for 4-5 minutes. The brew can be poured into cups through a nylon or metal strainer, or add cold water to the pot to help settle the grounds to the bottom. Eggshells can be added further to urge the grounds to their descent.

In France, where the idea of steeping coffee originated in 1711, a cloth bag containing the grounds was placed in the coffeepot and boiled water poured over it. The bag and grounds were lifted out of the brew in 3-4 minutes. This is similar to the present-day use of the cafézinho bag in Brazil.

Cold Water Method: Coffee grounds are steeped in cold water for 12-24 hours. The brew is filtered through a strainer. The extract is added to hot water although it tends to be quite a mild brew.

The Plunger Pot Method: The plunger is essentially an open-pot method except the coffee pot has a plunging apparatus to force the grounds to the bottom of the pot. The French Melior (marketed in 1920), the German Bodum, and the American Insta-Brewer pots which have recently been on the market use this method. A plunger combined with a metal or nylon filter attached to the coffeepot lid acts as the strainer. The cylindrical container for the steeping coffee is often made of glass and can be quite attractive, even extravagant looking, in some models.

Add the coffee grounds (medium grind) to the glass cylinder and pour in freshly boiled water. Allow to steep for 4-5 minutes. Place the plunger lid over the coffee/water mixture and push down, bringing the grounds to the bottom. Pour into cups immediately, as the coffee will cool quickly. The coffee brew tends to be rich in sediment and slightly bitter, which is usually more preferable in France than America. The advantage of this pot is that there aren't any filters to replace. The disadvantage is that the glass container is easily broken.

A plunger pot.

A de Belloy drip pot.

THE DRIP POT

The next method in coffee-making history was percolation (the drip method), by which hot water passes through the coffee grounds once and then into a second container. The term *percolation* is often erroneously associated with the pumping percolator, which passes water through the grounds several times. The drip coffeepot, known as the *perculateur* in France, was invented in 1800 by Jean Baptiste de Belloy, archbishop of Paris. This inspired Count Rumford, an American eccentric and scientist, to develop a ramming device to distribute the coffee evenly in the filter container.

The de Belloy pot consists of three parts: a cylindrical pot for hot water, a container for coffee grounds, and a cylindrical pot for the finished brew. These parts stack on each other and are still commonly used.

Method: Preheat the pot by scalding with hot water. Measure drip grind coffee into the filter section and place under the upper pot. Place the upper section with attached filter on the lower section. Pour freshly boiled water into the upper section and cover. After the water drips through the coffee grounds into the lower section, remove the upper section of the pot. All drip coffee should be stirred before serving.

The major disadvantage of these pots is that they are often made of aluminum, which interacts with the acid in the coffee.

NAPOLETANO (ITALIAN) OR CAFE FILTRE (FRENCH)

These are variations of the de Belloy drip pot, developed in the early 1800s. The Italians strongly identify with the Napoletano (also called Machinetta); however, the credit for this invention belongs to the French in 1819.

The coffee maker consists of two cylindrical pots, one with a spout and one with an escape valve. Between them is a compartment with metal screens on the top and the bottom. The advantage of this pot is that the method to heat the water is contained within the same pot.

Method: Fill the bottom half of the pot with cold water to just below the escape valve. Insert the metal filter and fill with coffee grounds (medium-fine or fine grind). Screw on the top of the filter, then screw on the other part of the pot over the filter with the spout facing downward. Heat on a medium heat until steam leaks from the escape valve. Turn the pot over and turn off the heat. The water drips through the grounds to the spouted pot. Stir the coffee and serve. As with drip coffee, the brew will contain sediment.

PUMPING PERCOLATOR

The pumping percolator was invented in 1827 by Jacques-Augustin Gandais, a Parisian jeweller. The device allowed water to rise through a tube inserted in the handle and spray down over the coffee grounds. In that year, Nicholas Felix Durant modified Gandais's percolator so that a central tube raised the boiling water, spraying water repeatedly over the grounds. It was readily adopted by Americans and is still typically used today. With so many other coffee makers on the market to choose from, perhaps the percolator's popularity can be attributed to the aroma of the coffee during brewing. However, with every gurgle of the percolator more aroma and the delicate oils vaporize, escaping into thin air rather than later being savored on the taste buds.

Method: Measure fresh cold water into the pot; the water level should always be below the basket. Measure the appropriate amount of fine grind coffee into the basket and then place the basket on the central tube and cover with basket lid. Then cover percolator with its own top lid. Heat until the water begins to bubble into the top, which can be viewed in the glass bubble on the lid. Reduce the heat. When the water becomes amber, allow to percolate gently for 5-6 minutes. Serve in cups or mugs. The resulting brew has acids predominating and a slightly bitter taste.

THE NAPIER VACUUM METHOD

This scientific-looking device was first developed by a Scottish marine engineer, Robert Napier, in 1840. It is quite a dramatic way to prepare coffee, often described as an alchemist's preparation. The original device consisted of a silver globe, a mixing container, a syphon, a strainer, and a gas burner. A variation on this theme that became popular after World War I was the Cona vacuum. It had two glass globes that stacked one on top of the other and a filter latched onto a tube.

Method: If using this coffee maker, fill the upper globe with fine ground coffee. Pour cold water into the lower globe and place on heat (gas or Bunsen burner). Fill the upper globe's cotton or mesh filter with a measured amount of medium fine grind coffee. Place over the lower globe and twist to seal tightly. Bring to a boil. The steam pressure forces the water up to the upper bowl, agitating the grounds. Stir well. Turn

A vacuum device.

The Melitta drip coffee maker.

Electric drip machine.

the heat off, allowing the pot to cool down. After a minute or two, the vacuum created by the cooling temperature of the lower bowl will pull the brew through the filter to the lower globe in a dramatic way complete with sound effects. This production lends itself to preparing it at the table or at a counter in view of coffee drinking guests. Remove the funnel and serve. This coffee maker produces a good brew; however, preparing coffee this way is time-consuming and the apparatus is difficult to clean up. In restaurants in Thailand, a vacuum-type coffee maker is used.

FILTER COFFEE

For those who prefer a clear coffee free of oils and sediment, filtered coffee is the answer. The cloth or paper does absorb oils, so if you like more body to your coffee, other methods are recommended.

Relatively recent arrivals on the market are coffee makers that use a paper filter. In 1941, the Chemex, a hand-blown glass coffee maker in the shape of an hourglass, was produced. It used a cone-shaped filter. In the 1960s, the Germans began marketing the Melitta with a wedge-shaped pocket filter. The coffee brew produced is a clear and flavorful liquid, similar to that from other filtered coffees. The advantage of the paper filters is that it is easier to prepare the coffee and clean up afterwards. This was the main reason why the vacuum method subsequently declined. A disadvantage of paper filters, however, is that they absorb the coffee's flavorful oils. Recently, there has been some concern over the chemicals created in the process of bleaching the paper, which could leave residues in the brew. Oxygen-bleached filters and reusable gold filters have been marketed to alleviate these concerns. Filters come in various sizes: individual filters for single cups and larger filters for oversized jugs.

Method: Use a very fine grind for your filter to provide maximum-quality coffee. Pulverized coffee will clog up the filter and coarse grounds will allow the water to run through them too quickly. Insert a filter into the filter container. Measure the very fine ground coffee (1-2 tbsp. per cup or less). Pour half the amount of boiling water over the coffee grounds. Allow the first liquid to drip through and then add the rest of the water. Remove the filter, stir, and serve.

ELECTRIC DRIP MACHINES

The electric drip machine was first made for restaurant use in the 1950s. Later, in the 1970s, it became a standard home-brewing device. The heating element on the machine is set to regulate the water temperature and the brewing cycle time (ideally 4-6 minutes), which will extract the desired aromatic substances from the coffee grounds and leave the other harsh elements. However, manufacturers seldom succeed in doing this; the most reliable success has been with machines using a higher wattage. The coffee produced in these machines is quite good. Another problem with this machine is that the coffee often stays on the burner too long (i.e., longer than 10 minutes), which changes any good coffee to a poor one. A *carafe,* an insulated pitcher that is airtight, is a good solution to the problem of overheating coffee on a burner. After the brewing cycle is complete, transfer the brew immediately to a carafe.

COFFEE BAGS

Coffee bags are a relatively new commodity to the market. Roasted and ground coffee is contained in individual sachets, just like tea bags. They are easy to use and dispose of.

Method: Boil water and allow to sit for 2 minutes to cool. The ideal water temperature for extracting coffee is just below the boiling point. Pour into a coffeepot or individual coffee cup. Add 1 coffee bag per cup of hot water. Allow to steep for 4 minutes. Remove coffee bag and serve.

ESPRESSO MACHINES

In the early 1900s, the Italians modified the French filtration pots. These espresso machines provide a unique method of brewing coffee using steam pressure.

Moka: The simplest of these devices is the Italian-made Moka. During the 1950s, the Moka began to be popular for home use. These aluminum or stainless steel coffee makers are placed over direct heat. The water in the base is boiled and then forced up by pressure through a metal filter basket containing fine ground coffee. This is the least expensive way to prepare espresso coffee.

Method: Fill the bottom container of the Moka with cold water up to the safety valve. Insert the coffee filter and fill it with espresso coffee, forming a mound in the filter. Do not tamp down. Screw on the top of the filter, then screw on the upper half of the pot tightly and place over a medium heat. Water is drawn up through the filter into the upper chamber. Enough pressure is created to brew the coffee before the water boils. As soon as you hear the spurts into the top of the coffee maker, turn the heat

Moka.

Atomic model.

An antique espresso machine.

A modern espresso machine.

to low, otherwise the water will boil. A high temperature of water (232 degrees) extracts the bitter flavor from the coffee. Espresso should be a heavy brew, strong and yet smooth. Other fancier stove-top models such as the Atomic and the Vesuviana work on the same principle and have a milk steamer for cappuccino. Moderately priced electric espresso machines actually work in the same fashion.

Espresso Machines: These were designed for cafes to brew coffee quickly. "Espresso" is derived from the Italian verb "to put under pressure" and refers to the steam pressure used in this brewing method. Early machines featured an array of spigots, valves, and handles and could turn out up to two thousand cups of coffee per hour. Unfortunately they tended to over-extract and scald the coffee, increasing bitterness. Since World War II, most of these machines have been replaced by electric and countertop versions. One popular model was invented in 1946 by Achille Gaggia. These machines improved blending of steam and hot water, which is pushed by pressure through the coffee grinds. Espresso machines require a finer grind and yield a smooth yet strong, rich, heavy-bodied brew. Most home espresso machines consist of a water reservoir, a receptacle to receive the coffee extracted, a metal filter basket for the coffee grounds, and a steam nozzle for milk on the side or top. True espresso has *crema,* a layer of light-colored foam, which you can only get with a piston or pump machine models that are capable of producing more pressure. The Pavoni uses a piston method that is activated by pulling a lever. The Pump machines have two switches: one for the heating element and one for the brewing cycle.

Method: Use a standard espresso roast, Italian or French—preferably a low-acid coffee as this process tends to increase the acidy taste of the coffee. You can try a lighter roast if you prefer and still obtain the heavy body of espresso, although it will lack the authentic tang. Use a standard coffee measure of finely ground coffee per demitasse cup. Place coffee grounds in the filter basket, filling to the brim, and tamp the grounds lightly and evenly. It is very important to have the grounds level. One common mistake is letting too much water through the grounds, which results in a thin bitter brew. This is due to either having too coarse a grind or not packing the grounds down enough. You may need to experiment with how hard you tamp down the grounds and how fine the grind is to obtain the perfect balance so the water passes through the grounds slowly. Fill the water receiver and heat pot on a burner. The presence of crema shows that the water has passed through properly. The richest espresso will come out at the beginning and the harsher chemicals at the end. Some people turn off the heat when the brew dripping out is becoming weak and thin-bodied.

Steaming Milk: Fill a pitcher half-full with cold milk (never hot). The steam jet is a pipe that protrudes from the machine. It has a screw knob for opening and closing it. Open the steam valve slightly and insert the nozzle in the pitcher of milk. Thrust the steam valve approximately 2/3 of the depth of the container into the milk and open up the valve more so you can hear the hissing of the steam. Then bring the nozzle just below the surface of the milk, gently moving the pitcher up and down slightly. When milk is steamed properly, milk foam will begin to rise in the pitcher. After you have achieved a good head of foam you can thrust the nozzle deeper to heat the milk if it is still cool. Keep pressure of steam moderate to low. Combine the steamed milk with espresso coffee, spooning the foam onto the top of the coffee.

A modern domestic espresso machine.

The Art of Making
the Perfect Cup of Coffee

The following tips will serve as a guide to brewing the perfect cup of coffee.

1. Preferably, buy the freshest coffee beans, which you can grind just before use. Try blending your own combinations. Coffee beans retain their flavor for up to three times longer than ground coffee. If you don't have a grinder, buy freshly ground coffee, only in small quantities sufficient for one week.

2. Store coffee in an airtight container, preferably glass, as coffee will absorb unwanted flavors. In fact, ground coffee is used to absorb odors in trucks that haul fish. Roasted coffee beans will keep for up to three weeks in the refrigerator and for a few months in the freezer provided that the container is tightly sealed.

3. Ensure that your coffee maker is clean of any residual oils. Wash in hot sudsy water and rinse thoroughly with hot water. The coffee maker should heat the brewing water to the ideal temperature of 200 degrees, plus or minus 5 degrees, for optimal extraction from the coffee grounds.

4. Make sure that you use the appropriate grind of coffee recommended for your coffee maker (see Roasts and Grinds chapter).

5. Ninety-eight percent of coffee is water, so the quality of water used deserves attention. Always use cold water for brewing. Cold water contains a small amount of dissolved oxygen, which hot water lacks; therefore the latter has a flat taste. Many municipalities add chlorine or other chemicals to tap water, giving it an artificial taste. Filtering devices can help remove these unpleasant off-tastes, or bottled spring water can be used. The water should have a small amount of dissolved minerals. If no minerals are present, such as with distilled or softened water, the coffee brew will taste bitter.

6. Use the recommended ratio of coffee grounds to water according to the coffee maker's instructions. For a medium-strong cup of infused or drip coffee, use a standard coffee measure (2 level tbsp.) per 6 oz. (3/4 cup water). Double the amount of coffee if using a steam-pressured device. Of course, preferred strength will vary based on the coffee drinker's experience and geographical location. The International Coffee Organization recommends, for a North American's taste, using at least 3 oz. of ground coffee for every 64 fluid oz. of brewing water. For the United Kingdom, it recommends 3.7-4 oz. of coffee per 64 fluid oz. of water, 4-4.7 oz. of coffee for Scandinavian countries, and 5.4-6.7 oz. of coffee for France.

7. Make only as much coffee as you need and serve immediately. Remove grounds promptly so that bitter oils are not extracted into the brew. Don't let the pot sit over heat for longer than 15 minutes as coffee will become bitter and have a burnt taste. If necessary, transfer coffee to a preheated thermal carafe. Never reheat cold coffee, as it destroys coffee's flavoring elements.

8. Choose your preferred size of cup. Avoid tin, styrofoam, or cardboard cups, which add off-flavors to the coffee. Prewarm your coffee cup with boiling water for a longer-lasting hot cup of coffee.

Coffee and Your Health

An understanding of the chemistry of coffee isn't necessary to enjoy a cup; however, for those who crave details or are health conscious, this chapter will be of interest. Coffee is composed of about eight hundred chemical compounds that produce its distinctive aroma and taste. These components range from common compounds such as carbohydrates (25 percent), proteins (13 percent), and water-insoluble fiber (35 percent), to special compounds such as oils (13 percent), acids (8 percent), ash (4 percent), and caffeine (1 percent in arabica and 2 percent in robusta). Although coffee contains protein, it has no nutritional value.

Caffeine is an organic alkaloid. Because the caffeine content of beans varies from 1.0 percent to 2.6 percent, the caffeine in a cup of coffee varies. Also, the degree of roasting affects the caffeine content, with higher roasts like espresso having less caffeine. The brewing method also yields variable amounts of caffeine. For example, in a 5-oz. cup the drip method has an average of 115 mg. of caffeine, whereas the percolator has an average of 80 mg. and instant coffee has an average of 65 mg.

There is extensive literature today on the effects of caffeine on the body. Although caffeine has been labeled as a mild stimulant acting on the central nervous system, scientists now believe that its action is not that direct. A recent widely accepted theory holds that caffeine effectively blocks receptor sites of certain neurotransmitters, specifically adenosine. This results in blocking the adenosine's action as a natural sedative that encourages the brain and the body to slow down. In other words, caffeine fools the brain into staying in high gear. Caffeine also interferes with the actions of certain drugs such as pain-killers and some antidepressants.

When consumed on an empty stomach, caffeine reaches body tissue within ten minutes and peak levels are reached in one-half hour. Caffeine does not accumulate in the body and is normally excreted within a few hours after consumption. Pregnant women do tend to retain caffeine in the body for up to three times as long as usual for adults. In contrast, heavy smokers clear caffeine from the body twice as fast as non-smokers. Caffeine acts to constrict blood vessels and therefore is a common ingredient in some medications for migraine headaches. It also slightly increases the body metabolism, blood pressure, and kidney action. Both regular and decaffeinated coffees have a mild laxative effect.

Whether it's an early-morning java or a late-afternoon latte, people look to caffeine for a hearty boost of energy, a sharpened mental alertness, and enhanced performance. People's sensitivity to caffeine varies greatly. Some individuals experience insomnia if they drink coffee late in the day; others are not affected. In sensitive people or in high doses caffeine can lead to nervousness, anxiety, irritability, and gastric disturbances. Some suggest that caffeine affects people depending on their personality type. It may improve extroverts' performance on tasks that demand constant careful responses more than it helps introverts. Despite the many generations of writers who attest to thinking more clearly because of coffee, coffee does not gift us with more intellectual capacity. Some tests have shown improved speed on simple motor tasks such as typing but reduced performance on tasks requiring fast coordinated reactions. Contrary to popular belief, caffeine beverages will not help an individual sober up from excessive alcohol consumption.

Nowadays most foods and beverages have been subjected to "scientific" studies to determine what their long-term effects are on the health of consumers. Coffee is no exception. Although studies have suggested that too much caffeine can cause everything from infertility to heart troubles, all these studies have been contradicted or are methodologically flawed. For example, in the early 1970s, one study found a high association between heavy coffee drinking and increased heart disease. However, this study was misleading because the confounding factor of cigarette smoking was not qualified. Longitudinal studies have since found no link between caffeine intake and heart disease, angina, or severe arrhythmias. Studies examining a possible association with various types of cancer have to date been inconclusive.

In 1980, the FDA advised pregnant women to avoid caffeine consumption, after a study in which pregnant rats were force-fed extremely high doses of caffeine, pumped directly into them via a stomach tube. They subsequently gave birth to offspring with missing toes. Later, rats were fed equivalent dosages of coffee orally in drinking water with no resulting birth defects. No human studies have found birth defects. Erring on the side of caution, most doctors advise pregnant women to limit their caffeine intake.

Although far more subtle than cocaine or nicotine, caffeine is considered by some experts to have the classic features of an addictive drug: it can induce cravings and cause withdrawal symptoms. The most common symptoms are headaches and fatigue; some people also experience insomnia and irritability. Regular caffeine intake can produce a tolerance for its effects. The first cup of coffee can really wake up a person. More caffeine within the hour may not have much of the same impact, whereas three hours later the effects of caffeine would be noticeable again. However, unlike drugs of dependence, coffee does not require steadily increased doses, it is not associated with antisocial behavior, and it is not difficult to stop.

Most of the major health risks have been ruled out; however, research continues on at a steady pace. In the face of conflicting data, both the FDA and the American Medical Association (AMA) agree that moderate coffee drinkers probably do not need to be concerned about health hazards assuming that their life-styles are otherwise healthy. Coffee has been on the list of GRAS (generally recognized as safe) substances since 1958. Our motto is that quality not quantity of coffee is the key to one of our last truly forgivable indulgences.

Coffee Recipes

The coffee brew is steeped with many traditions. As it spread around the world, each country contributed its own unique rituals to coffee drinking. We hope that the following recipes will allow you the opportunity to partake in the wide variety of coffee customs from around the world in the comfort of your own home.

Traditional Coffee Recipes

ARABIA

Coffee drinking is a prominent element in Arabic social life and provides a gesture of hospitality towards one's guests, who participate in the ritual by accepting two or three cups. The Arabs have a saying: "The first cup is for the guest, the second cup for enjoyment, and the third cup for the sword." A cup of coffee is essential at any social or business gathering. It is considered an insult not to offer a visitor coffee soon after he/she arrives. The consumption of alcohol is strictly forbidden and therefore coffee is the acceptable social drink here.

The coffee beverage was originally prepared using fermented coffee berries and water and thus its name *Kawah*, which means wine spirit in Arabic. When coffee spread through Europe it retained that reference as the "wine of Araby." Around A.D. 1000, they began roasting the bean. The standard way of preparing Arabic coffee is the same as Middle Eastern countries (see "Turkish Coffee" in the Brewing Methods chapter) with some local variations. The coffee beans are roasted to a shiny black and then pulverized very fine with a mortar and pestle (*tahrini*). The coffee is then boiled with water and sugar in a long-handled pot called a *rakwi* or *jaswah*. Early accounts of coffee making in this area do not mention the use of sugar being added, so it appears to be a variation adopted at a later time. The coffee is served sweet (*mazboutah*) or very sweet (*hilweh*). Coffee without sugar (*murrah*) is very rarely brewed. The coffee is sipped from earthenware demitasse cups. There are two boiling methods that are common: the Bedouin method (like the Turkish method) and Mazboutah method.

BEDOUIN METHOD

4 demitasse cups cold water
Sugar (4 tsp. for *mazboutah*, 8 tsp. for *hilweh*)
4 heaping tsp. pulverized coffee (dark roasted)
2 split pods cardamom
1 tsp. ginger (optional)

Put the water and sugar (as preferred) into a rakwi and bring to a boil. Remove from heat and add coffee, cardamom pods, and ginger (if desired). Bring to a boil again. When the foam rises to the top, remove from heat. Repeat this process two more times, allowing the coffee to rise to the top each time.

Note: Often cardamom, ginger, or other spices are added to coffees from Middle Eastern countries.

Serve in demitasse cups (small 3-oz. cups). Sip slowly, allowing the coffee sediment to settle. Serves 4.

MAZBOUTAH METHOD

4 demitasse cups cold water
4 heaping tsp. coarsely ground coffee (dark roasted)
2 split pods cardamom
Sugar (4 tsp. for *mazboutah*)

Put water, coffee, and split cardamom pods in a long-handled rakwi or jaswah and bring to a boil. Reduce heat and leave to simmer for 15 minutes. Serve in demitasse cups. A teaspoon of sugar is added to each demitasse. Serves 4.

KAWAH-MURRAH

Flavored with cardamom and saffron.

2 tsp. pulverized coffee
2 demitasse cups water
1 crushed cardamom pod
1 tsp. saffron powder

Combine ingredients in a rakwi or small saucepan, stir, and bring to a boil. Reduce the heat and simmer for 20 minutes until coffee is reduced. Then add only a small amount of sugar to taste. Serve in demitasse cups. Kawah-Murrah is slightly bitter tasting. Serves 2.

ARMENIA

Khahue or *soorj* (coffee) is prepared in a long-handled conical Turkish ibrik called a *soorjaman*. The method of preparation is the same as the "Turkish" method. A common addition to coffee is a couple of drops of orange-blossom water, which are added at the same time that the pulverized coffee is added. Coffee is served after dinner and on social occasions.

AUSTRALIA

Nescafe instant coffee has been firmly established in Australia's and New Zealand's coffee-drinking habits and, for special occasions, so has percolated coffee. Coffee is served white (with cream) or black.

BILLY COFFEE

In the outback, a billy (a large can with a wire handle) is filled with water and ground coffee is added. The billy is placed over the fire and brought to a boil, then removed from the heat to steep for about 10 minutes.

AUSTRIA

In 1683 the first coffeehouse, the Blue Bottle, was opened in Vienna by Franz Georg Kolschitsky. Milk and honey were added to filtered coffee.

A long-standing unique custom in the Austrian *Kaffeehaus* (coffeehouse) is that a glass of water is served simultaneously with the cup of coffee. A waiter comes around to the table to refill the water glasses at intervals. Patrons are allowed to stay in a *Kaffeehaus* drinking cupful after cupful of coffee as long as the water glass still needs emptying. It is believed that the long hours patrons have spent sitting and drinking coffee may be the reason so many works of art have been created in Austrian *Kaffeehauses* over the years.

During World War II, the Austrian *Kaffeehaus* owners had on their hands a "coffee serving" dilemma of moral proportions. Coffee was in short supply and so was people's money. The *Kaffeehauses* couldn't make a profit by serving continuous cups of coffee for so little money in return. At the same time, the proprietors did not want to change their custom of serving *Kaffee* by the cupfuls all day long. The problem was eventually resolved by the government stepping in and subsidizing coffeehouses so they could survive during this financially difficult period.

The modern-day *Kaffeehaus* (no longer subsidized) contains pool tables and a wide variety of global newspapers. Patrons can rest, sip coffee, catch up on world events, and perhaps create a work of art!

KAFFEE MIT SCHLAG
(COFFEE WITH WHIPPED CREAM)

> **4 cups cold water**
> **4 tbsp. fine ground coffee (Viennese roast)**
> **Whipped cream**

In a large saucepan, heat water and coffee grounds. Bring coffee to a boil. Lower heat, cover pot, and simmer for a few minutes. Remove from heat. Let coffee grounds settle and strain coffee into coffeepot. Serve with milk. Top coffee with gobs of whipped cream *(Schlagobers)*. Serves 2-4.

KAFFEE WEISSER

> **1 cup hot milk**
> **Strong freshly brewed coffee (Viennese roast)**

Serve hot milk in cups. Add a splash of coffee to each cup. This is really a hot milk drink with a slight coffee taste. Serves 1.

GETROPFTER KAFFEE (DRIP COFFEE)

> **1/2 cup medium grind coffee**
> **2 tsp. grated orange rind**
> **1/4 tsp. ground cinnamon**
> **1/2 tsp. brandy extract**
> **4 1/2 cups cold water**
> **Honey and cream to taste**

Place coffee grounds and grated orange rind in filter basket of a drip coffee maker. Sprinkle cinnamon and brandy extract over the coffee mixture. Add boiling water to the coffee maker and drip through. Serve in cups. Add honey and cream as desired. Serves 4.

WIENER KAFFEE (VIENNESE COFFEE)

Austrians love coffee topped with whipped cream.

2 cups hot drip coffee
1/4 cup whipped cream
Grated orange peel
Cinnamon and nutmeg

Serve coffee in demitasse cups. Drop a dollop of whipped cream on top of each serving of coffee. Garnish cream with freshly grated orange peel, cinnamon, and nutmeg powder. Serves 2-4.

BELGIUM

CAFE LIEGEOIS

A specialty of the city of Liège.

1-2 egg whites
1 cup heavy cream, whipped
Sugar to taste
4 cups hot coffee (dark roast)

Beat egg white(s) until stiff. Fold into whipped cream. Add sugar to taste. Half-fill cups with sweetened meringue cream mixture and fill the remainder of the cups with hot coffee. Sweeten with sugar to taste. Serve each person with a square of Belgium chocolate. Serves 4.

CAFE BELGE

Make the above Café Liègeois recipe. Add 1 tsp. vanilla extract to cream when whipping. Add vanilla cream to cups before filling them with coffee. Serves 4.

Brazil is the largest producer of coffee in the world. Brazilians themselves are known to drink as much as two dozen cups of coffee a day. In cities such as Rio de Janeiro and São Paulo, steaming coffeepots, with sets of porcelain cups and saucers, and bowls of damp sugar are carried on shiny trays through offices, in homes, and on the streets. Except for breakfast coffee, the brew is drunk jet black from demitasse cups. At breakfast larger mugs are used for coffee with milk.

The busy working-class Brazilians slip into *poderias* (stand-up coffee bars) for glassfuls of coffee during the day. Men are often served two glasses—one with coffee and the other with *pinga,* a sugarcane liqueur. Customarily, the pinga is thrown back first in one gulp followed by the cafézinho. So ends the coffee break and off they dash, back to work.

Brazilians take a great interest in new coffee-making pots. However, they often return to their favored and time-honored method of making coffee with a cotton filter bag, referred to as a cafézinho bag. The bag is a conical shape with wire running through a top hem to hold it open in a circle. Brazilians insist that the bags are best after they have been used a few times. Brazilian coffee is usually made of the best grade of Santos, roasted dark brown and ground to the fineness of granulated sugar.

CAFEZINHO BRASILEIRO

Drip method: Hang the cafézinho bag (see "Steeping" in the Brewing Methods chapter) down inside a pot. In a separate pan, measure 4 oz. of cold water per serving and bring to a boil. Put one standard coffee measure per serving plus one for the pot into the cloth bag. Pour boiling water over the bag, and allow it to drip through the coffee grounds. Serve in small cups.

Steeped method: Measure the same amounts of coffee and water. Use a coarser grind and set bag in pot so the boiling water surrounds it. Allow to steep for 5 minutes. Serve as desired (see recipes below).

CAFE PRETO (BLACK COFFEE)

Fill the demitasse cup almost to the brim with damp sugar (available in Brazil), which melts extremely quickly compared to hard granulated sugar. Fill the cup with strong black coffee and serve immediately.

CAFE COM LEITE

Besides coffee plantations, Brazil has a large dairy industry.

Hot Brazilian coffee (see above)
3 cups hot milk
Sugar to taste

Place 3 oz. of brewed coffee into each large cup or bowl and fill with steaming hot milk. Sugar to taste. Café com Leite is served at breakfast. Serves 4.

CAFE DE BAHIA

This is an area in Brazil that has a strong African influence dating back to slave trading. There are many coffee plantations here.

1 1/2 cups water
1 1/2 tbsp. sugar, or to taste
4 tbsp. pulverized coffee

Heat water and sugar in a saucepan to just below the boiling point. Stir in the coffee, heating gently for a few minutes, but *do not* allow to boil. Remove from heat and let steep for 1 minute, then pour coffee through a cafézinho bag into a warm coffeepot or pitcher. Serve in demitasse cups.

CAFE BRASILEIRO COM CHOCOLATE

2 cups brewed coffee
1 oz. (1 square) unsweetened chocolate
3 tbsp. sugar
Dash of salt
1 cup milk
1/2 cup cream, whipped

Heat coffee and chocolate in saucepan on low heat, stirring continuously until chocolate is melted. Add sugar, salt, and milk and continue to heat until very hot. Stir continuously. Remove from heat and whip with a beater until mixture is bubbly. Serves in demitasses. Top with whipped cream. Serves 6.

CAFE PICANTE BRASILEIRO
(SPICED BRAZILIAN COFFEE)

Add 3/4 tsp. cinnamon powder and 1/4 tsp. allspice to Café Brasileiro com Chocolate.

CAFE FRIO DE COPACABANA (ICED COFFEE)

1 oz. (1 square) unsweetened chocolate
1 1/2 tbsp. sugar
1/2 cup strong hot coffee
1 1/2 cups milk, scalded
Ice cream

Melt chocolate in the top of a double boiler over high heat. Stir in sugar to dissolve. Pour hot coffee slowly into chocolate mixture, stirring continuously. Add scalded milk to coffee mixture and warm on lower heat for 5 minutes. Remove from heat and whip with a beater until frothy. Pour over cracked ice into tall chilled glasses. Top each with a large scoop of ice cream. Serves 2.

CANADA

Mainstream coffee drinking in Canada is similar to that in the U.S. We prefer a light- or medium-roast Colombian coffee. Our coffee is most often perked with regular grind coffee. Since the 1970s, Melitta coffee makers and Bodum plunger pots have become more popular. The majority of Canadians buy vacuum-packed ground coffee in cans or boxes. Coffee bars are becoming more popular, introducing the large variety of coffee beans and preparations, particularly Italian style. Coffee is served black or straight (without cream or sugar), light (with milk or 10 percent butterfat cream), with cream (light cream or 50 percent cream and 50 percent milk is added), or light with sugar (1 tsp. of white or Demerara sugar added to light coffee).

RIVERBANK COFFEE

4 cups cold water
1/2 cup coffee (regular grind)
1 egg, beaten
1 tbsp. water
Dash of salt
1/4 cup cold water

Bring 4 cups water to a boil in a large pot. Combine coffee, egg, 1 tbsp. water, and salt in small bowl, mixing well. Add coffee mixture to boiling water. Boil for a few minutes, stirring occasionally. Remove from heat and pour 1/4 cup cold water over coffee mixture to settle grounds. When grounds are settled, serve in coffee mugs. Serves 4.

CARIBBEAN

Coconuts are more common than cows in this area so coconut milk is often used instead of dairy milk in morning coffee.

ESENCIA DE CAFE

As in many Latin American countries a strong coffee essence is used in preparing coffee.

1 cup ground coffee (medium ground, dark roast)
1 1/4 cups boiling water

To prepare the coffee extract place coffee in coffee drip basket. Add boiling water 1/4 cup at a time. Let drip slowly until all water is added. Store coffee essence in a glass jar with seal-tight lid. Refrigerate and use when desired.

CAFE NEGRO

A black after-dinner coffee.

1 1/2 to 3 cups boiling water (depending on strength desired)
1 cup Esencia de Café

Add boiling water to coffee extract and serve in cups. *Alternative:* Individuals preferring their coffee at different strengths can add their own desired amount of coffee extract to their cups.

CAFE CUBANO

2 cups cream or coconut milk
1/2 cup coffee (fine ground, dark roast)
Sugar to taste

Combine cream or coconut milk and coffee in a pan. Heat but do not boil. Strain through fine-mesh sieve into coffee cups. Sweeten with sugar to taste. Serves 2.

CENTRAL AMERICA

Throughout Central America, coffee is often not brewed fresh. Rather, a cold coffee essence (extract) is added to hot milk or hot water. Coffee essence is brewed using four times as much ground coffee to the same amount of water, as is called for in any other coffee brewing method (drip, boil, perk).

ESENCIA DE CAFE

8 standard coffee measures
2 cups hot water

Prepare coffee as dictated by the type of coffee maker. To serve add 1-2 tbsp. coffee essence to cup of hot water depending on strength desired.

CAFE DE PILON (BROWN-SUGAR COFFEE)

1/2 cup dark brown sugar
4 cups water
4 tbsp. pulverized coffee

Dissolve brown sugar in boiled water. Add pulverized coffee and simmer for 1 minute. Allow coffee to stand for a few minutes until the grounds are settled. Pour into demitasses. Serves 8.

COLOMBIA

AGUA PANELA (Colombian Coffee)

If you ask for *agua panela* in Colombia, the locals will know you want a coffee. When Colombians separate their coffee beans for export, the large good beans go out of the country and the small beans are kept for the locals. Colombian coffee isn't made with straight water, but with sugarcane water. A sugar water is first made by putting sugarcane pieces into water and boiling until the water is sweet. When the water is sweet, 2 tbsp. coffee grounds are added, then the pot is covered, the heat is turned off, and one waits until the coffee grounds settle. The sweet coffee is then carefully poured off the top of the pot into glasses. Sometimes the coffee liquid is filtered through a cotton filter into another pot or into the cups. Colombians believe the older and more coffee-stained the filter is, the better the flavor of the coffee.

When you order *café* in a restaurant, the coffee brand is usually Castilla or Sello. You ask for "tinto"—regular black coffee with sugar. Colombians usually drink hot chocolate for breakfast and "only" 3-4 cups of coffee a day.

DENMARK

The Danes have an early supper hour. In their longer evening hours, they can enjoy socializing, while sipping their rich-flavored cups of Kaffe Copenhagen or Kaffe med Fløde (coffee with cream) to their hearts' content.

KAFFE COPENHAGEN

3 1/2 cups hot coffee
1/2 cup rum
1/3 cup sugar
1 stick cinnamon
6-8 whole cloves

Combine all ingredients in a saucepan. Heat mixture over a medium heat. Ladle into cups. This coffee can be kept warm on a very low heat for up to 1 hour while dinner is being served. Serves 4.

EGYPT

Early accounts describe Egyptians as liking their coffee strong and unsweetened. Later the addition of sugar was adopted, and in Egypt today, coffee is preferred strong but sweet.

The Egyptians have distinctive and sanctioned rules of etiquette that they adhere to when serving coffee. Persons of high social status and the elderly are always served first. Then, traditionally, men are served before women. Coffeehouses are frequented by men only, giving them a retreat from the everyday hustle and bustle. Customarily, one man prepares the coffee, serving it in clear demitasse cups. Another man will ensure that patrons have a *sheesha* (water pipe) filled with tobacco. A patron can sip coffee, puff on the sheesha, play backgammon, chess, or checkers, or sit back and contemplate the beauty of the Nile.

In most Middle Eastern countries, the coffee drink resembles mud and it really is surprising that a spoon does not stand up in it. Dark-roasted mocha beans from Yemen are popular. The coffee is prepared by the "Turkish" or "Arabic" method. You have to specify how much sugar you want in your coffee or you will automatically receive a very sweet drink:

Kahwa ziyadda: ultimate sugar dose, i.e., extra sweet.

Kahwa mazbouta: moderately sweet.

Kahwa saada: without sugar.

Coffee can be flavored with cardamom or saffron, which is added at the same time as the pulverized coffee. The coffee cup is perfumed with the smoke of mastic or the fragrance of ambergris for a special occasion.

An Egyptian coffee vendor.

EL SALVADOR

A culturally interesting phenomenon that stands out about El Salvador is that Salvadorians drink *instant* coffee called *Café Listo* while this is a country of well-established coffee plantations. Salvadorians believe they must drink instant coffee so that the best coffee beans may be exported. Plantation workers and poorer Salvadorians make their coffee by boiling leftover coffee-bean husks and filtering the brew through a cloth or metal filter. This coffee is called *café molido*. Bags of coffee-bean husks, whole or ground, may be purchased at the market. Even in urban areas of El Salvador the coffee-drink choices are the same.

A story from an acquaintance has it that poorer Salvadorians may serve café molido in baby bottles to their youngest ones. Older children are given their coffee in a cup. Salvadorians do not drink their coffee with milk. It is often drunk from the half-shell of the morro fruit. The cup is called the *guacal de morro,* meaning the container that is made out of the morro fruit.

Coffee is drunk black *(café negro),* or black with brown sugar *(negro con azúcar).* White sugar or panela may be served instead of brown sugar. Panela is brown sugar that comes pressed in a cone shape. The user flakes off the amount of sugar he/she desires with a knife or other utensil.

CAFE DE MAIZ

Corn kernels are dried and ground. The ground corn is then roasted. Place the corn grounds in a pot. Add hot water and boil until Café de Maíz is a coffee-brown-colored liquid.

ENGLAND/GREAT BRITAIN

Oxford claims to be the first place where coffee was drunk in England in 1635. By 1673, London alone had over three thousand coffeehouses. Coffeehouses were at their peak in the seventeenth century and became places to discuss business, politics, literature, and the arts. Coffeehouses later became taverns and coffee drinking declined in favor of tea, probably because tea was easier to prepare. England now is renowned as a tea-drinking nation. However, since 1950, there has been an increased interest in coffee. Coffee bars have made a comeback. The British have a reputation for drinking pale watery brews, usually prepared with a percolator. Recently the use of coffee bags has become quite popular, probably because of their similarity to tea bags, and their ease of preparation (see the Brewing Methods chapter).

When it comes to cream, the English have the rest of the world beat. England differentiates double cream, heavy cream, single cream, and cream. Even their single cream is rich in butterfat compared to that from other countries. Today English coffee is served black (no sugar or cream), white (with cream), or white with sugar (cream and sugar).

FINLAND

The Finnish people are reputed to be some of the heaviest coffee drinkers in the world.

KAHVI

1 egg, well washed
3 tbsp. coffee
4 cups boiling water

In a medium-sized pot, crush an egg (shell and all) and mix it with the coffee grounds. Add the boiling water to mixture in pot and bring to a boil. Remove from heat, letting coffee settle for a moment, then return to heat and bring to boiling point again. This process may be repeated a third time, if desired. Cover pot and allow grounds to settle. It is the eggshells that help in clearing the coffee. Serve coffee by pouring it off the top of the pot into glasses or cups, or pour coffee into a copper coffeepot first when serving formally. Serves 4.

Variations: Kahvi Mustana (black coffee), Kahvi Maidan Kera (coffee with milk), Kahvi Kerman Kera (coffee with cream).

FRANCE

The French prefer a dark-roasted coffee with a distinct bitter taste and a heavier sediment. Drip pots (café filtre) and the Melior (plunger) pot are commonly used. In France, boiling or reheating coffee is a definite *faux pas*.

CAFE NOIR (AFTER-DINNER COFFEE)

By 1687, the custom of drinking coffee after dinner was firmly established.

Prepare a strong brew using 3 tbsp. coffee for each cup of water. Serve in demitasse cups. In many regions in France, coffee is served with a "splash" of alcohol (see "Traditional After-Dinner Coffees" for Café Chantilly, Café au Marc de Bourgogne, Café Royale, Café Normandie, and Café au Rhum).

CAFE AU LAIT

A delightful morning ritual in France and Quebec is to have a bowl of café au lait with fresh croissants to leisurely start the day. Café au lait is a student's drink, where they can get some nutrition and alertness to fuel their long studying hours.

1 cup scalded or steamed milk
1 cup strong hot coffee (medium roast)
Cinnamon powder (optional)

The coffee and milk should be the same temperature. Combine the milk and coffee in a large bowl. If café au lait is made with steamed milk, after the liquids are combined, spoon the froth that remained in the milk jug onto the coffee. Sprinkle with cinnamon if desired. Serves 1 or 2.

CREME CHANTILLY
(SWEET AND FLAVORED WHIPPED CREAM)

To make crème Chantilly, add approximately 4 tsp. sugar to 1 cup heavy cream before beating. Regular beet sugar, vanilla sugar, or confectioners' sugar may be used, depending on your preference for sweetness.

Beat heavy cream and sugar by moving beaters (electric or hand-held) around mixing bowl, allowing lots of air into the cream. Crème Chantilly is whipped when the beater leaves light traces on the top of the cream.

Crème Chantilly may be hand-whisked. It is whipped to completion when the cream forms light soft peaks. It will cling to the whisk when the whisk is raised from the bowl.

A chilled crème Chantilly is made by using chilled heavy cream and placing the mixing bowl with cream in a container of chilled water and ice cubes when beating. *Cream whips best when chilled.*

Variations: add 4 tsp. sugar to the following flavored crème Chantilly recipes unless otherwise specified:

Chantilly à la vanille: add 1 tsp. vanilla extract per 1 cup heavy cream when whipping. This is a good cream to add to Café Belge.

Chantilly au café: add 1 tsp. finely powdered instant coffee or 1 tsp. powdered espresso coffee to 1 cup heavy cream when whipping.

Chantilly au cacao: add 1 tsp. cocoa powder along with extra sugar to heavy cream when whipping.

Chantilly avec cacao et café: add 1/2 tsp. coffee powder and 1/2 tsp. cocoa to heavy cream when whipping.

Chantilly au goût de liqueur: add 1 tsp.-1 tbsp. of your favorite liqueur (Triple Sec, Grand Marnier, Kirsch) to heavy cream when whipping. Create the taste sensation you desire.

Chantilly au cognac: add 1 tsp.-1 tbsp. of the finest cognac to heavy cream when whipping.

Note: Heavy cream doubles in bulk when whipped. These recipes may be halved or doubled.

CAFE AU VIN

4 tsp. sugar
1 tsp. ginger powder
1/2 cup sweet red wine, warmed
4 cups Café noir
4 tsp. orange juice
1/2 tsp. coriander powder

Add sugar, ginger, and wine to hot coffee. Pour into 4 coffee cups. Add 1 tsp. orange juice to each cup. Dust the top of each drink with coriander powder. Serves 4.

GAMBIA

The following is a recipe of the poor people in Gambia, who cannot afford prepared coffee. Their coffee is imported from Senegal or the Ivory Coast. Gambians prepare a huge pot of coffee in the morning for the whole family to accompany the *ndeewoo* (breakfast) of bread and butter.

CAFE

3 cups coffee beans with shells
2 large pots
Fire

Put coffee beans in pot and place on the fire. When the pot is hot, the black shells will crack and break up releasing the coffee. When you are sure all the shells have broken, remove from the fire and let cool for 10 minutes. Place a light wire screen or net over the pot. Sift the coffee through the screen, into second pot, so the shells can be discarded. In the second pot there should be 1 cup shelled coffee beans for every 4 people. Add water for number of people having coffee. Heat coffee mixture approximately 10 minutes.

In Gambia, these versions are enjoyed:

Café ak sukur: coffee with 1-2 tsp. sugar.

Café ak mew: coffee with a little milk.

Café niul: black coffee (this is most popular).

Wahtu café: coffee break is at 11:00 for white-collar workers. Ground coffee is added to heated water in a *flash* (large flask) that is kept in the office.

The German people prefer filtered coffee. It began in 1908, when Melita Bentz filtered her coffee through a linen towel. Afternoon coffee, which had its beginnings with the Kaffeeklatsch where affluent ladies exchanged gossip, continues today. Pastries and torte are the favorite accompaniment with coffee.

KAFFEE MIT SCHLAG

Top lightly roasted coffee with whipped cream.

KAFFEE MILCH

Same as café au lait (France). Serve in a bowl at breakfast.

EIGELB KAFFEE (EGG COFFEE)

2 egg yolks
1 tbsp. honey
2 tbsp. brandy
2 tbsp. cream
1 1/2 cups hot coffee

Combine the egg yolks, honey, and brandy and beat until frothy. Spoon the froth into 2 cups. Add the cream and hot coffee. Serves 2.

BAYRISCHER KAFFEE (BAVARIAN COFFEE)

4 egg yolks
4 tsp. fine sugar
2 cups hot strong coffee (dark roast)
1 cup milk, scalded
Granulated sugar
1/2 cup warmed brandy (rum optional)

In a double boiler over hot water, whisk egg yolks and fine sugar until threads drip from the whisk when it is lifted up from the mixture. Slowly add coffee, milk, and granulated sugar while whisking continuously. When heated, stir in warmed brandy. Serve in warmed goblets or cups. Serves 4.

GREECE

The dark-roasted, finely ground Greek coffee *(kafedaki)* is traditionally prepared in a long-handled conical pot called a briki using the standard "Turkish method" of preparation. Coffee is served in demitasse cups either plain *(sketos)*, medium sweet *(metríos)*, or very sweet *(glyko)*. The foam *(kaimaka)* created during the first rising of boiling coffee is usually skimmed off the top and placed in the demitasse cups. The Greeks take special care in making sure they have kaimaka covering the coffee as it is a disgrace to the host to serve it without. A *kafetzou* (fortune-teller) will be able to forecast your future from the patterns made by the remaining coffee grounds if you invert your cup after finishing your drink. In Greece, it is not unusual to observe elderly men sitting about for hours at the local taverna, chatting or playing tavali (backgammon) and sipping cupful after cupful of coffee.

KAFEO

Follow the "Turkish method" of boiling the coffee mixture three times.
Variations:
Plain (sketos): 1 demitasse cup water, 1 tbsp. Greek coffee.
Medium sweet (metríos): add 1 tsp. sugar.
Sweet (glyko): add 2 tsp. sugar.
Greek coffee is typically served with one or two glasses of cold water on the side.

GUATEMALA

In Guatemala, coffee is drunk black *(café negro)* or with lots of milk added *(café con leche)*. Coffee may be drunk sweet using granulated white sugar or a brown sugar flaked off a sugar cone called panela (see El Salvador and Venezuela).

Coffee grounds are put into a pot of cold water and heated. When the coffee reaches the boiling point, the pot is taken off the fire or stove and poured through a cloth filter into another pot. From this second pot, the filtered coffee is poured into cups. Guatemalan cups are made of clay *(tazas de barro)*.

In local eateries, coffee is made in a pot, the same way it is done at home. The European coffee machines have yet to become part of mainstream Guatemalan coffee culture although a good restaurant may boast an espresso machine. To date, there aren't any coffeehouses or cafeterias in Guatemala where the main purpose of the establishment is to serve coffee or coffee and snacks to its patrons.

Breakfast coffee is café con leche served with tortillas. Children drink an even milkier coffee. As in most Latin American countries, children start drinking coffee at a young age. During the afternoon, about two o'clock, Guatemalans take time off from their activities or jobs for what they call *una hora de café* (an hour for coffee).

HUNGARY

Like Germans, Hungarians enjoy a medium to full roast with chicory blended in. Scalded milk is added and whipped cream is used for a special treat in the afternoon or evening.

TEJESKAVE (BREAKFAST COFFEE)

For breakfast, Hungarians drink a half-milk, half-chicory-coffee mixture. A tablespoon of chicory is added to the coffee grounds to stretch the coffee further and to deepen its flavor.

1/2 cup freshly brewed chicory coffee
1/2 cup scalded milk

Pour coffee into cup to half-full. Fill the rest of the cup with milk. Serves 1.

UZSANNAKAVE (AFTERNOON COFFEE)

Add 2 tbsp. chicory powder to the coffee grounds when making this coffee.

2/3 cup hot chicory coffee
1/3 cup hot milk
Whipped cream

Pour coffee and milk into a cup. Top with whipped cream. Serves 1.

FEKETEKAVE (FESTIVE COFFEE)

For festive occasions, Hungarians drink extra-strong filtered coffee without chicory added. Serve in demitasse cups.

JEGESKAVE (ICED COFFEE)

Pour strong black coffee over ice.

ICELAND

In Iceland, the coffee is usually prepared using a drip method. Serve in cups and add cream. A sugar cube is customarily placed under the tongue while sipping coffee.

INDIA

Coffee was planted in India by a Moslem pilgrim in approximately 1670. Although India is a tea-drinking nation, the coffee-drinking custom is well established in the southern areas. Coffee is roasted and ground fresh every day, and is usually served in a brass coffeepot.

Coffee powder is used in preparations. It is made by pulverizing roasted coffee beans with a mortar and pestle. The coffee is sifted through a fine sieve and used like an instant coffee. The name for black coffee is *bi-naa doodh*.

THAN DI KAAFEE (COLD COFFEE)

2 1/2 cups milk
1 tbsp. coffee powder
3 tsp. sugar
Cracked ice

Boil milk in a pot. Add coffee powder and sugar and stir. Allow coffee mixture to cool. Add cracked ice. Pour into blender and whip at medium speed until foam forms on top. Serve coffee in glasses. Serves 2-3.

HADHALI KHAND KAAFEE (PALM SUGAR COFFEE)

Palm sugar is made from the sap of various palms, and can be found in any store specializing in East Indian food.

1 cup water
Palm sugar
2 tsp. pulverized coffee powder
Scalded milk

Boil water and sugar in a pot. Add coffee powder and milk to taste and heat for a few more minutes. Serve in a glass. In India coffee is drunk from plastic glasses. It is sometimes difficult to obtain pasteurized milk in the rural areas of India, so milk must be heated to the scalding point when used. Serves 1.

INDONESIA

Coffee beans were first planted in Indonesia by Dutch colonists around the year 1687. Indonesia became famous for Java coffee, so much so that in England a cup of coffee was referred to as a "cup of java." After the war, however, with many plantations destroyed, the arabica bean was replaced by the planting of robusta beans. It is now difficult to come across the same "java." Today, coffee is grown on the islands of Bali, Flores, Java, Portuguese East Timor, Sulawesi (Celebes), and Sumatra.

There is nothing as inviting as a *kopi warung* (coffeehouse or hut) in Indonesia. It is a small thatched hut, usually about three meters square, fit with a long bench and counter. About five to seven customers can occupy the warung at one time. Once you sit down and order, the waiter does the rest. He makes your coffee in front of you, complete with adding sugar and/or cream and stirring it for you. Kopi in the warungs is served with snacks like fried tofu, *krupuk* (chips), *kue* (cake), and Tempe Goreng.

KOPI SATU OR KOPI KENTAL

Roasted Sumatran coffee is finely ground and used like instant powdered coffee. To a cup, a waiter adds the Sumatran coffee powder, 2 tsp. sugar, and cream or sweetened condensed milk (no sugar needed).

Hot water is added, the coffee is stirred by the waiter, and the patron sits and chats with other customers for a few minutes while waiting for the grounds to settle.

Kopi Cap Kapal Api is a condensed-milk trademark name, but often customers who want their coffee with sweetened condensed milk order their coffee using the trademark name. The name has become synonymous with the coffee drink itself.

Kopi Susu is coffee with cream (with or without sugar).

KOPI JAHE (GINGER COFFEE)

Indonesians have developed a taste for a sweet ginger-water coffee.

5 thin slices peeled ginger
4 cups water
4 tsp. powdered coffee
Sugar to taste

Heat ginger and water in a pan by bringing water to a boil. Lower the heat and simmer for 10-15 minutes. Remove ginger from the water. Place 1 tsp. powdered coffee in each cup and pour hot ginger water over top. Add sugar to taste. Stir. Serves 4.

KOPI LUAK OR KOPI TUBRUK

A small catlike animal called a *luak* enjoys gorging on ripe coffee berries during the night. It digests the fruit and then expels the beans in the morning. The locals collect, wash, and roast the beans. They claim that the natural fermentation that occurs in the luak's stomach makes this a distinct delicacy in coffee drinking. Those brave souls in search of a new taste will have to travel to Indonesia to experience this brew, as we are sure it is not exported.

IRAN

Iranians are mainly tea drinkers. However, many people may indulge in a demitasse of Turkish coffee a day.

GAHAVEH OR GHAHVE

2 tbsp. pulverized coffee grounds, dark roast
1 cup water
1 tsp. sugar (optional)

Add to briki and boil twice. See ''Turkish Coffee Method'' in Brewing Methods chapter. A large pot of black coffee is made for parties/funerals.

IRELAND

IRISH COFFEE

Probably one of the most popular after-dinner coffee drinks in the Western world.

1 1/4 cups whipping cream, sweetened
1 1/2 cups Irish whiskey
6 tsp. sugar, white or Demerara
4 cups black coffee (preferably French medium roast)

Whip cream with sugar to taste. Pour 1 jigger of whiskey into each preheated goblet. Add 1 tsp. sugar to each. Fill goblets with hot coffee to 2/3 full, stirring to blend and dissolve sugar. Spoon a dollop of whipped cream onto each coffee. Serves 6.

Warming glasses or goblets: Irish coffee is best served in warmed goblets. Warm goblets by swishing boiling water around in them just before use.

Sugar-frosting goblets: The glass rim of the goblets may be sugar-frosted by holding each glass upside down and dipping the rim in a liquid, such as lemon juice, coffee liqueur, or whiskey. If using lemon juice, take a wedge of lemon and rub lemon juice all around the inside and outside rim of the goblet for about 1/4 inch from the top of the rim down. Then dip the moistened rim in superfine sugar.

ISRAEL

CAFFA SHABAT (SATURDAY COFFEE)

On Saturday, religious Israelis are not allowed to cook, so they prepare their food on Friday night. Water is heated on Friday night in a large urn called a *plata*. On Saturday, Israelis may drink coffee by adding 1 1/2 tsp. fine-grind powdered coffee to each cup of preheated water. Sugar (*sokar*) may be added to the coffee.

In Israel, Turkish coffee is drunk in small glasses. For large pots, 2 heaping tsp. well-ground coffee are added for each 3/4 cup water in the pot. Measure coffee and water for how many people are drinking coffee. Boil three times (like Turkish coffee on a big scale).

In the 1950s, Italian coffee makers became popular in bars and restaurants. The Italian espresso machines are being exported throughout Europe. Southern Europeans have drunk strong coffee in demitasse cups or mixed coffee with hot milk for generations. Most of the espresso drinks commonly made are not original in concept to the machine itself; however, the machines do add excellence to the drinks produced. Currently, fine-ground Italian-roast coffee is gaining popularity in North America.

Italy is a land for coffee drinkers with an assortment of choices. Usually *caffe latte* is enjoyed in the morning. The small demitasse cups of espresso, available in the many stand-up espresso bars, keep the momentum of the day going. Cappuccino is another option for those who prefer a milky and frothy version.

ESPRESSO ITALIANO

This well-known beverage is made with very dark pulverized coffee often brewed in the two-tiered Machinetta or Moka pot. It is also prepared in espresso machines. Refer to Brewing Methods chapter for more details.

> 8 tbsp. Italian-roast coffee (very fine grind)
> 1 1/2 cups water

Make according to directions of coffee maker. Serve in demitasse cups with sugar to taste. Serves 3-4.

ESPRESSO ANISETTE

Flavor a demitasse of espresso with a few drops of anisette.

ESPRESSO ROMANO

Serve a demitasse of espresso with a thin slice of lemon. This seems to be an American addition.

ESPRESSO CON PANNO

Garnish espresso with whipped cream.

CAPPUCCINO (MONK'S COFFEE)

The name comes from the color of the drink, which is the same as the attire of the Capuchin monks. A cappuccino coffee maker has a tube with a nozzle that pushes steam into the neck, heating the milk and raising a light froth on top. It is necessary to have a steamer to make this recipe.

1/3 cup espresso coffee
1/3 cup steamed milk
1/3 cup foam from steamed milk
Chocolate slivers (optional)
Ground cinnamon and nutmeg (optional)
Sugar to taste

Place espresso coffee in cup, then pour in steamed milk. The steamed milk will pour out of the pitcher, leaving foam behind. Spoon the milk froth onto the coffee-milk drink. Top with chocolate and/or spices if desired. Sugar to taste. Serves 1.

CAFFE LATTE

This mixture contains an equal amount of hot or steamed milk and espresso coffee. It is commonly enjoyed at breakfast.

1/2 cup espresso
1/2 cup hot or steamed milk

Serve in bowl or wide-mouthed glass. Serves 1.

LATTE MACCHIATO

1/4 cup espresso
3/4 cup milk

Fill a glass 3/4 full with hot foamed milk. Trickle a demitasse of espresso over the back of a spoon so it will color the milk in graduating layers, lighter towards the bottom. A slightly lower temperature of the milk relative to the coffee is important for this to layer. Spoon more foamed milk on top of the espresso layer to make a third layer. Serves 1.

MOCA (MOCHA)

Voltaire supposedly drank up to fifty cups of mocha a day.

1/3 cup espresso
1/3 cup strong unsweetened hot chocolate
1/3 cup steamed milk
Sugar

Combine espresso, chocolate, and steamed milk in a cup. Add sugar as desired. Mocha is a mixture of coffee and chocolate flavors. Serves 1.

CAFFE MOCACCINO

1/2 cup chocolate milk, heated
1/2 cup hot espresso coffee

Combine ingredients. Serves 1.

CAFFE BORGIA

The Borgias were a powerful, aristocratic family in Italy from the second half of the fifteenth through the sixteenth centuries. Known for their cruelty and bloodletting, the Borgias were much hated by their fellow Italians. The most notable Borgia was Pope Alexander VI. In need of revenue for the Vatican, he made money by marrying off his niece, Lucrezia (1480-1519), to rich men. He then ordered her husbands to be murdered one after the other, keeping their wealth for the Vatican coffers. A story has it that Martin Luther was on the steps of the Vatican when the pope's henchmen tried to kill Lucrezia's fourth husband. Unfortunately, the husband did not die right away but instead lingered on in a hospital for a time. During Lucrezia's visits to her dying husband, she learned of the way in which her other husbands had met their demise. So disheartened and overwhelmed was she by this discovery that immediately after her last husband's death, she entered a convent. Eventually Lucrezia escaped the powerful control of her evil uncle by committing suicide. As for Martin Luther . . . well, there is no doubt that his revolutionary Protestantism was fuelled by his observance of the Roman clergy's corruption.

1/2 cup hot espresso coffee
1/2 cup hot chocolate
2 tbsp. whipped cream, lightly sweetened
1/2 tsp. grated orange peel
1 tsp. bittersweet chocolate shavings

Combine coffee and hot chocolate in a cup. Top with whipped cream. Sprinkle orange peel and chocolate shavings over top of whipped cream. Serves 1.

CAFFE CIOCCOLATA

1/2 cup hot or steamed milk
1/2 cup hot espresso coffee
Whipped cream
1/8 tsp. ground cinnamon
Shaved semisweet chocolate
Sugar

Combine hot milk and espresso in a cup. Top with whipped cream. Sprinkle cinnamon and shaved chocolate over the cream. Add sugar to taste. Serves 1.

JAPAN

On almost *every* street in Japan, vending machines provide sweet cold and hot coffee. Hot imported coffees—Brazilian, Nicaraguan, Guatemalan, Kenyan—are also available in vending machines. The vendee does best to scout the neighborhood to find the machines that will deliver his/her favorite indulgences.

Sumiyaki coffee is finding its way into the *kinaten* (restaurants) these days. However, not all Japanese know yet what it is. Coffee beans are roasted on charcoal fires, ground fresh, and used in the coffee maker to make Sumiyaki *kohii*.

The Japanese are still fond of the vacuum coffee maker. Spectacular vacuum coffee makers of incredible sizes that serve a crowd can be seen in many restaurants. Often the gigantic coffee makers are not in use, but they serve as part of the decor or as an artifact on display in the kinaten.

Small gas-heated vacuum coffee makers are commonly used to make coffee for one or two. Coffee drinking in Japan is *takai* (expensive). In most public places in Japan it is considered that one doesn't pay just for the coffee, but for the privilege of the space one is taking up while sipping.

Kuriimu (cream) often is not cream in Japan. It is a vegetable extract made to approximate cream. *Kohii* (coffee) is drunk the same way as coffee in the U.S.A. and Canada—kuriimu and *sato* (sugar) are added. The amount added is up to the individual. When it comes to instant coffee, Nescafe Gold Blend has made its way into many a Japanese household and workplace.

LIBYA

LIBYAN QAHWAH

In eastern Libya coffee is often flavored with cardamom (2 seeds per cup) and 1/2 tsp. powdered saffron. The sugar is omitted. The French café au lait (coffee with milk) is often served in Libya as well.

MACAO

This colony was settled by the Portuguese for approximately 440 years. Menus are still written in Portuguese, although only 3 percent of the population is of Portuguese descent. About 95 percent are Chinese. Macao will be returned to China in 1999.

CAFE PESQUELA (SMALL COFFEE)

A strong espresso coffee served in a demitasse.

CAFE GRANDE

Strong coffee in a large cup, served the same way as in North America. Sugar and cream may be added to taste.

CAFE PICANTE COM GUSTA A MAÇA (SPICY APPLE COFFEE)

Coffee
5 whole nutmegs
1 apple slice, 2 in. wide
1 cinnamon stick
Whipped cream

Fill a long-stemmed glass 3/4 full with coffee. Embed nutmegs in apple slice. Float the apple slice on top of the coffee and insert a cinnamon stick. Top with whipped cream.

MALAYSIA

About 90 percent of the population drinks coffee. Malaysians of Malay, Chinese, and Indian descent all prefer their coffee sweet, thus coffee is always served with sugar. Coffee is grown locally in the Cameron Highlands. The standard versions are:
Kopi "O": coffee without milk (has 2 tbsp. sugar).

Kopi Suso: coffee with milk (2-3 tbsp. condensed milk with 2 tbsp. sugar or sweetened condensed milk without sugar added).

Kopi Besah: plain coffee.

Kopi Peng (iced coffee): fill glass with ice cubes and pour Kopi "O" or Kopi Suso over.

KOPI PENANG

In the small villages of Penang, coffee is roasted charcoal black and then coarse ground. Hot water is poured through coffee in a cloth filter set in a pot resembling a tin can with a handle. It is heated on a fire stove 8-10 minutes. The filter and grounds are then removed. Even though drugs are highly illegal in Malaysia, it is a Chinese custom for the elders to place a small ball of opium below the coffeepot. The fumes of the opium waft through the air while the coffee is prepared. Needless to say, when the elderly men return from their work, they settle down in the local *kedai* (coffee bar), where they relax for hours.

UNCANG KOPI CAMPURAN (COFFEE MIXTURE BAG)

Malaysians can purchase their coffee in coffee bags, like tea bags in the West. The coffee is medium ground, medium to dark roast. The freeze-dried coffee bags come in a variety of mixtures: coffee, powdered mixture, fine sugar; coffee, cocoa, sesame powder and margarine (most common); and a superior-quality, rich mixture, 80 percent coffee, 20 percent sugar and margarine. Add boiling water, let sit for 2 minutes, and serve coffee.

MEXICO

Mexicans brew a medium-bodied coffee with beans that are dark roasted to a mahogany black with shiny coating. The beans are often roasted with sugar.

CAFE DE LOS CABOS

1/2 cup regular-roast coffee
1/4 cup dark-roast coffee
1 tsp. ground cinnamon
2 tbsp. cocoa
6 cups boiled water
Sugar and cream

Combine coffee grounds in basket of drip-style coffeepot. Sprinkle cinnamon and cocoa over top of grounds. Add water to coffee maker and brew. Serve hot. Add sugar and cream as desired. Serves 6.

CAFE D'OLLA

Mexican pot coffee—boiled method.

4 cups water
1/2 cup Mexican coffee beans, coarsely ground
2 sticks cinnamon
2 tbsp. brown sugar
1 tsp. molasses (optional)

Combine ingredients and bring to a boil. Reduce heat for a few minutes, then bring to a boil again. Reduce heat and simmer for a few more minutes. Serve. Serves 4.

CAFE MEXICANO DEL CAMPO
(RURAL MEXICAN CAFE)

A stronger and sweeter version of Café d'Olla.

4 cups water
4-5 oz. piloncillo (unrefined cane sugar) or substitute 1/2 cup packed
**   brown sugar plus 1 tsp. molasses**
1 cinnamon stick
2/3 cup dark-roast coffee, medium to coarse grind

Combine water, sugar, and cinnamon in pot. Bring to a boil. Stir in the coffee and remove from heat. Cover and steep for 5 minutes. Remove cinnamon stick and pour coffee into earthenware cups. Serves 4.

CAFE CON LECHE

Coffee with milk, very common in Mexico.

Combine equal amounts of coffee and hot milk in cups. Drop a cinnamon stick into each drink.

CAFE MEXICANO

1 cup milk
2 oz. semisweet chocolate (2 squares)
1 tbsp. sugar
1/4 tsp. almond extract
1/4 tsp. cinnamon
1 cup strong coffee (2 tbsp. ground coffee per cup of water)
2 cinnamon sticks

Heat milk and chocolate in saucepan over a low heat, stirring constantly until chocolate melts. Do not boil. Add sugar, almond extract, and cinnamon. Mix with a fork for 10-15 seconds. Fill 2 earthenware mugs half-full with chocolate mixture. Top with hot coffee. Serve with cinnamon sticks as stirrers. Serves 2.

MOROCCO

Coffee arrived in North Africa (Algeria, Tunisia, Morocco, and Libya) during the occupation of these lands by the Ottoman Turks in the seventeenth century. Turkish coffee was introduced and is still popular in these areas.

QAHWAH

Qahwah is traditionally prepared in a small brass pot *(jazoua),* following the Turkish method of boiling three times. In Morocco, qahwah is usually cooked without sugar, which is added at the end. Add 1 or 2 drops orange-blossom water just before or after removing from the heat the last time. A pinch of cinnamon can be added along with the coffee.

MOROCCAN QAHWAH

Sometimes this spice mixture requires a little bit of work to put it together. A homemade variation we use is to mix 1 tsp.-1 tbsp. (for 8 cups coffee) of the spice called "Chinese Five Spices" with the coffee grounds in the filter basket, before making drip coffee. "Chinese Five Spices" actually has seven spices in it: anise, cinnamon, cloves, fennel, ginger, licorice, and white pepper. It is a nice combination of pepper and sweet spices. Check the spice shelves of your local grocery store and see if you can come up with something similar.

> 8 rose hips
> 1 tsp. aniseed
> 1 tsp. ground cardamom
> 1 tsp. ground cinnamon
> 1/2 tsp. ground cloves
> 1 tbsp. ground ginger
> 1 tsp. ground mace
> 1 tsp. nutmeg
> 1 tsp. ground black peppercorns or white pepper

Crush rose hips in mortar with pestle or grind fine. Combine with other ingredients. Store in a glass jar with a good seal. Add 1/4 tsp. per 4 standard coffee measures of ground coffee. Prepare coffee as per coffee maker.

NEPAL

In this traditional *chiya* (tea) drinking nation, coffee is considered a treat. It is sometimes the drink of the wealthier, or of those who could afford imported coffee for a special occasion.

KAAFEE

When company comes.

Prepare a coffee paste using 3 tsp. strong coffee (fine espresso), sugar (1 cup), and a little hot water. Spoon 1-2 tbsp. coffee paste into a cup filled with hot milk or 1/2 cup hot water and 1/2 cup hot milk. Stir. Milk *(dudh)* in Nepal is not pasteurized so it must be heated for a while to sterilize it.

COFFEE MILK

The Nepali like their coffee and tea milky.

Add powdered instant coffee to a glass of hot milk. It is considered rude to serve tea or coffee without sugar. When company comes to visit, if you want to impress them or express how much you like them, you make sure the coffee is served very sweet; symbolically, the sweeter the coffee or tea the more the host likes or respects the guest.

MILK-TEA COFFEE

For a special coffee.

Add 1 or 2 tsp. powdered instant coffee to milk tea. Milk tea is made by making 1/2 glass hot, strong tea in the usual way and then adding 1/2 glass scalding hot milk. Sugar is added to make the coffee sweet.

THE NETHERLANDS

In 1663 milk was first used in coffee to reduce what drinkers thought was a bitter taste. The Dutch, recognizing the potential of coffee, started growing coffee in Java in the seventeenth century and managed to break the well-guarded monopoly of the Arabs. Coffeehouses sprung up in Holland and are still a tradition today. The Dutch prefer a medium roast, usually prepared by the drip method.

KOFFIE MET KANEEL (CINNAMON COFFEE)

1 long cinnamon stick
1 cup black coffee (dark roast)
1 tbsp. heavy cream
Sugar
1/2 tsp. butter (optional)

Place cinnamon stick standing up in a coffee cup. Pour in hot coffee. Stir in cream and sugar to taste. Float butter on top of coffee. Koffie met Kaneel can be made without the butter. Serves 1.

Variations: Zwarte Koffie (black coffee), Koffie met Melk (coffee with cream).

Norwegians often place one or two sugar lumps *(sukker)* in their mouths and sip the coffee, slowly dissolving the sugar. Milk is added according to preference.

To request *kaffe,* ask for:

Kaffe uten fløte: coffee without cream.

Kaffe med fløte: coffee with cream.

Kaffe med sukker: coffee with sugar lumps.

En espresso: Espresso coffee made the same as in Italy.

KAFFE

Put regular grind kaffe (1/4 cup) into a copper coffeepot *(kaffekjel)* with 4 cups water and boil for a few minutes. Pour into porcelain cups. To make more kaffe, Norwegians just add more coffee grounds to the leftover coffee and old grinds in the pot. They add more water and boil again. The grounds may eventually build up to half a kettle of coffee grounds. These are finally boiled well to dispel the last essence of the coffee before dumping the old grounds for fresh ones. Serves 4.

EN KAFFEDOCTOR (BRANDY COFFEE)

To a cup of coffee, add a shot of brandy.

CAFE MACHU PICHU

Peru produces some excellent coffee in its mountain regions. They prepare a coffee essence that is made in a very small drip coffeepot designed for the purpose. The fine-ground coffee is placed in one compartment with a screen bottom. The hot water is poured over it and slowly drips through to the bottom compartment. The coffee essence (2-3 tbsp.) is poured into the cup and hot water is added. Peruvians like coffee with sweetened condensed milk added.

PHILIPPINES

Malayba Café (Negros) is no longer an export but grown for local use. Arabica plants grow at the foot of Kanlown Volcano, under the shade of acacia trees. Filipinos are not major coffee drinkers; however, coffee is usually served for breakfast and during the *Meriena* (3-5 P.M. siesta). It is accompanied by rice cakes *(Bibingka)*. Coffee is drunk black and sweet—loaded with unrefined sugar from their many sugar plantations.

KAPE

Boil 6-8 cups water in a pot with a few tbsp. regular-ground Malayba coffee. Filter through a mesh sieve into an aluminum coffeepot. Add 2 tbsp. sugar.
Kape Blanco: Add lots of sugar and a small amount of milk.

POLAND

In Poland, *Kawa Czarna* (black coffee) and *Kawa ze smletanka* (coffee with cream) are enjoyed.

PORTUGAL

Coffee is still imported from the former Portuguese-owned colonies of Angola and Brazil. Coffeehouses in Portugal have long been social gathering centers for men. These gatherings are traditionally leisurely affairs where books are read, and storytelling and conversing continues for hours over a cup of *café*. With the increase in tourists setting a trend, women have begun to infiltrate these longtime male institutions. Coffee is also served at *uma pastelaria* (cake shop) and snack bars, in the following versions:

Café: strong standard coffee, prepared in an hourglass vacuum pot in finer restaurants.

Bica: very strong coffee served in a demitasse.

Carico: a weaker brew of one-half strong coffee, one-half boiling water (American strength).

Galão (Café com Leite): strong filter coffee mixed with hot milk.

Galão Escura: strong coffee with a little hot milk.

Galão Claro: strong coffee with lots of hot milk.

Garato: milky coffee.

Café Gelado: iced coffee.

RUMANIA

The Rumanian method of making and drinking coffee is an assimilated mix of cultural habits between the Middle East and Europe.

CAFEA

2 tsp. pulverized coffee (dark roast)
2 tsp. fine sugar
1 tsp. cocoa
1 cup water
Cream and sugar to taste

Spoon coffee, sugar and cocoa into Turkish ibrik. Add water. Heat coffee mixture until the rolling boiling point when bubbles are forming and the mixture is rising up to the rim of the ibrik.

Remove from heat for a few seconds, then heat again until froth rises to the top of the ibrik. Pour into demitasses. Spoon the coffee froth onto the top of each demitasse. Serves 2. Recipe may be doubled depending on the size of your ibrik.

Like Europeans, Rumanians serve cream and sugar with their coffee. Each coffee drinker can add to his/her coffee the desired amounts of these.

KAPHE RUSSE

1-oz. square semisweet chocolate
1/2 cup sugar
1/2 cup water
Dash of salt
3/4 cup light cream
2 cups hot coffee, brewed strong
1 tbsp. vanilla extract
Whipped cream (optional)

Melt chocolate in the top of a double boiler. Stir in sugar, water, and salt. Simmer gently for 5 minutes, stirring constantly (use whisk). Add light cream and heat. Add coffee and vanilla extract. Beat with a rotary beater or whisk until foamy. Pour into glasses. Top with whipped cream, if desired. Serves 4.

SOUTH AFRICA

One would think that with coffee beans growing practically next door in Angola and Malawi, South Africa would have a coffee fare. Bring along your own coffee if you're traveling to South Africa because South Africans only seem to like instant coffee. Chicory powder, however, is added to some instant coffee brands.

SPAIN

In Spain, coffee drinkers say, *"Un café solo, por favor,"* if they wish to enjoy black coffee. They can also drink *cortada* (espresso with milk) and *café con leche* (coffee with milk).

QUEMADO DE LICOR

1 cup brandy or cognac
Sugar
2-in. stick cinnamon
2 slices lemon peel (1/8-in.-thick strip of the peel from pole to pole)
2 slices orange peel (1/8-in.-thick strip from pole to pole)
3 cups hot coffee (Spanish dark roast)

Heat brandy, sugar, cinnamon, and citrus peels in a ceramic dish. Ignite the mixture and flambé for 1 minute. Douse the flames with hot coffee. Ladle into earthenware cups. Serves 4.

SWEDEN

The Swedes start drinking coffee at a very young age and are heavy coffee drinkers. It is common to use a rock sugar that is cut with a special tile cutter into small pieces. A piece is kept under the tongue while sipping on coffee to sweeten the brew. Swedes also enjoy dipping a rusk (toasted sweet bread) into their coffee.

KAFFE

1 egg, lightly beaten (shell reserved)
3/4 cup regular coffee grounds
1/2 cup cold water
8 cups boiling water

Combine egg with coffee grounds. Mix in cold water. Crumble eggshell and stir into mixture. Add boiling water to coffee mixture. Heat on high heat until foam disappears (approximately 4 minutes).

Remove pot from heat, cover coffee, and let stand until grounds settle. Pour clear coffee off the top of the pot into cups or strain through a fine metal sieve into coffee cups.

SWITZERLAND

In Switzerland, coffee is often made with or served with chocolate.

HEISSER MOKKA (HOT MOCHA)

1/2 cup heavy cream
1/4 cup chocolate pieces
1 cup hot coffee

Blend the cream and chocolate pieces until liquefied. Pour in hot coffee; blend for 30 seconds. Serve with pieces of chocolate on a side dish. Serves 2.

KALTER MOKKA (COLD MOCHA)

3 oz. semisweet chocolate
1/2 tsp. cinnamon
2 cups strong coffee
Shaved ice
Whipped cream

In a double boiler, melt chocolate. Stir in cinnamon. Blend in coffee. Cool. Pour into 2 tall glasses, partly filled with shaved ice. Top each with a dollop of whipped cream. Serves 2.

SYRIA

It is believed people in Syria were serving coffee in petite cups as early as 1480.

SYRIAN DEMITASSE

4 cardamom seeds
1 cup hot coffee, strongly brewed (Turkish style)
Sugar to taste

Place 2 cardamom seeds in the bottom of each demitasse. Crush seeds with the rounded back of a spoon. Add coffee to each demitasse. Sugar to taste. Serves 2.

TAIWAN

Taiwan is a tea-drinking nation. Those who drink coffee usually drink instant Nescafe coffee. Coffee drinking is a new migration to Taiwan, since the 1970s. For many people, it is still considered a treat.

Coffee is always served sweet and with powdered milk (called *ten*). The small country of Taiwan doesn't have a dairy industry. When a Taiwanese acquaintance was asked what the Taiwanese do with the powdered milk lumps that don't dissolve in the coffee, she replied, "Coffee is drunk with the lumps in it." City students, businesspeople, and anyone who wants to hang out for long hours will do so at the *gabitias* (coffeehouses). Some upscale gabitias serve percolated coffee. Coffee cups are not in standard use in Taiwan. Coffee is drunk from glasses, cups, bowls, etc.

When ordering coffee in Taiwan you may ask for *gabi gulin* (Taiwanese) or for *kafei* (Mandarin-Peking dialect) or *gkoubpih* (Hokkien dialect).

TANZANIA

Tanzania (formerly Tanganyika and Zanzibar) produces a rich-flavored mellow arabica bean from the area of Bukoba. Even though it is a coffee-producing country, tea is the most common drink. Coffee is a cash crop, grown primarily for export. Naturally coffee is drunk more around harvest time as beans are available. It is also drunk in the colder months of June and July.

The beans are roasted and then ground in a mortar and pestle. The crushed beans are sifted through a wire-mesh sieve, keeping a medium-ground coffee. A native of Tanzania described the method of preparation as one of "eye and experience" rather than precise measurement.

KAWAH

3 cups water
1/4 cup coffee grounds
1 cup milk
1/4 cup sugar

Bring water to boil in a pot. Add coffee and bring to a boil for a couple of minutes. Add milk and sugar (Tanzanians prefer more milk for a richer taste and less sugar due to economics). Bring to a boil again. Pour into earthenware mugs. For guests, it is strained whereas for regular home use the grounds are left to settle in the cups. In Tanzania, they occasionally add a spicy peppery mixture similar to Morocco to their coffee grounds for a "hotter" brew.

THAILAND

In the preparation of Thai coffee, canned milks are used, as fresh dairy products have only been in use for a relatively short period of time. The Thai people usually prefer their *gha faa* (coffee) sweet and milky although the following are common variations:

Gha faa Dam: black coffee without sugar, typically served hot in a glass.

Gha faa Dam Ron: black coffee with sugar.

Gha faa Ron: hot coffee with milk. Canned evaporated milk is added to hot coffee.

Gha faa Yen: iced coffee with milk. Fill a tall glass with shaved ice and fill 2/3 full with a strong brew of hot coffee. Add sweetened condensed milk and swirl with a spoon. This has given rise to the term *dancing milk*.

Gha faa Dam Yen (Oliang): sweetened, iced black coffee. Fill a glass with shaved ice and add a strong brew of black coffee. Sweeten with sugar syrup, which is often served in a small pitcher on the side.

Nowadays, freeze-dried Nescafe is widely used in restaurants throughout Thailand. An electric thermos of water is plugged in so coffee is served in an instant.

GHA FAA DAM

Roasted coffee beans are finely ground and are often blended with other ingredients such as corn, sesame seeds, and rice, each adding a subtle unique flavor to the brew. The coffee is prepared by using a cloth bag made of muslin approximately 1 foot long, tapering from about 5 inches in diameter at the top. A metal ring with an attached handle keeps the top open. Coffee grounds are placed in the bag and boiled water is poured through it into a saucepan. Allow it to steep for 3 to 4 minutes. The bag is then placed in a second container and the brew is repeatedly poured through the bag of grounds, alternately using the two containers, until the desired strength is obtained (3-4 times). Lift the bag out of the brew, squeezing out any excess liquid. For a traditional strong brew, use 1/3 cup Thai coffee and 3 cups water.

TUNISIA

Tunisia, with its Mediterranean setting, is a country whose cuisine has been multiculturally influenced. The African, Arab, and European influences are exemplified in the many methods of preparing coffee absorbed into Tunisian everyday life. The number of names that Tunisians have for their coffee drink tells the story:

Kahwa (also referred to as Kahwa Arabic): coffee made with strong fine coffee powder.

Kahwa Arabi (also referred to as Café Turc): strong powdered coffee, but not as strong as Kahwa Arabic.

Café Express (Italian dark roast): same as Italian espresso.

Café Noir: black coffee.

The elderly people in Tunisia prefer Kahwa Arabic or Kahwa Arabi prepared in a *zazwa* (like a Greek ibrik) over a *kanoon*. A kanoon is a clay ceramic pot; a fire is made at the bottom of it, using charcoal for heating. Coffee powder, sugar, and water are added into the zazwa and coffee is boiled two or three times consecutively, removing the zazwa from the kanoon at the height of each boil when the *tanwa* (or coffee cream) foams at the top. The tanwa, considered the essence of the coffee, is spooned into the bottom of a demitasse before the Kahwa Arabic or Kahwa Arabi is poured in.

Drops of *zahr* (orange- or rose-flower water) are added to each coffee during serving. The orange drops are extracted from the flower of the sour orange tree. The oranges of these trees are too sour to eat so the flowers are boiled to make orange drops.

Kahwa Arabic uses a fine coffee powder that produces a strong taste, and is always made on the kanoon. Kahwa Arabi is in more general usage in Tunisia, most often being made on modern stoves. Kahwa Arabic and Kahwa Arabi are rarely drunk in the morning. These stronger coffees are enjoyed in the afternoon and early evening, served often with Tunisian treats such as baklawa (Turkish honey-pastry cake) and *ghraiba* (date paste and ground-wheat pastry).

Coffee is not grown in Tunisia. It is imported from the Ivory Coast in Africa and the Bahia area in Brazil. With the independence of Tunisia in 1956 came a wide variety of European-style coffees and coffee makers, particularly those of Italian and French influence. The French *cafetière* (percolator) is common in Tunisia.

Tunisians prefer a *m'khalta* (mixture) of coffee and roasted garbanzo beans as opposed to pure coffee, but the European-style coffees are now popular with young people and office workers.

These coffees include:

Café Noir: also known as Kahwa Kahla—black coffee.

Lait Tache: a small amount of milk is added to black coffee.

Café au Lait: also referred to as Kahwa Hlib or Kahwa Chtar, where the quantity of hot milk in the cup is the same as the coffee (see France).

Café Crème: the same as café au lait (see France), only the milk in the cup is steamed.

Capussin: the same as cappuccino (see Italy). This coffee is popular among the young and the young at heart.

Breakfast in Tunisia is European style, similar to what the world refers to as a Continental breakfast. In the mornings, Tunisians sit down to Kahwa with a croissant, cake, or breadlike snack.

TURKEY

Turkish coffee was popularized in Europe by the Turkish ambassador to France, who created a fashion in high society by serving it to his guests at exotic parties. A few years later, Pascal, an Armenian, sold the Turkish brew at the Saint-Germain fair in France with wonderful success. The Turkish custom is to drink coffee strong and sweet. Other Middle Eastern countries such as Lebanon, Cyprus, Iran, and Afghanistan prepare a Turkish-style coffee.

TURK KAHVE

1 demitasse water
Sugar
1 tbsp. pulverized coffee

Combine water and desired amount of sugar in the Turkish ibrik. Bring to a boil over a moderate heat. Add coffee, stir, and place over the heat. Allow the froth to rise up to the brim and then remove from the heat. Wait a couple of seconds and then return the pot to the fire until it rises again. Wait 2-3 seconds and repeat this procedure for a third time. Spoon off the froth and place in the demitasse cup. Pour the boiled coffee mixture into the cup. Sip slowly, allowing the sediment to settle in the bottom of the cup. Serves 1.

Note: Remember to brew no more than 6 cups at a time.

Variation: Add a couple of rose-water drops when the coffee is added.

When ordering coffee in Turkey, as in other Arab countries, one orders it by the degree of sweetness.

Şekerli: sweet.

Orta şekerli: medium sweet.

Az şekerli: slightly sweet.

Sade: not sweet.

UNITED STATES

The Americans are credited for bringing about the coffee break, for which we are all thankful. It is a time to take a pause from whatever activity you are involved in and enjoy just being there in the moment, relaxing with a cup of coffee. Coffee is an integral part of the whole day. America wakes up to aromas wafting from the percolator, looks forward to coffee breaks throughout the day, and often sits up late at night with one more cup of coffee.

It is believed that the Dutch first introduced coffee to America. Like the Dutch, the majority of Americans prefer milk or very light cream in their coffee. After the Boston Tea Party in 1773, coffee became a staple beverage in American homes. In 1908, Hill Brothers marketed the vacuum package for coffee, so ground coffee could be stored longer without losing its flavor. Although numerous pots have been used, from tin cans to glass vacuum pots, the pumping percolator is still used in 60 percent of the homes. With the American invention of the coffee mug, a couple more ounces could be consumed and saucers were done away with.

In the 1940s, two ex-servicemen, Lloyd Rudd and K. C. Melikain, invented the automatic coffee vending machine. Today the public vending machines are about as common as a postage stamp. These machines render a particularly bad brew of coffee; however, they seem to flourish. The selections are made by pushing a button for the desired combination and a paper cup is ejected to be filled with ingredients:

Black: strong coffee syrup with hot water.

THE COFFEE BOOK

Light: coffee with powdered milk.

Light with sugar: coffee with powdered milk and 1 tsp. sugar.

If you want an even worse tasting cup of coffee, two more buttons can be pressed simultaneously with the first selections:

Extra light: extra powdered milk.

Extra sugar: equivalent to 2 tsp. sugar.

PICNIC COFFEE

Tie 2 tbsp. coffee grounds (regular grind) per 1 cup water into a square piece of cotton cloth allowing for double expansion of the coffee grounds. Dangle the coffee bag in your saucepan of water. Bring the water to a boil three times, removing coffee from heat each time the boiling point is reached.

COFFEE EGGNOG

2 eggs, well beaten
2 tsp. instant coffee
4 tsp. sugar
2 cups chilled milk
1/4 tsp. vanilla extract

Whip ingredients in a blender until the mixture develops a light froth on top. Serves 2.

COFFEE ICE-CREAM SODA

2 tsp. instant coffee
2 tbsp. milk
Vanilla, coffee, or chocolate ice cream
1 bottle ginger ale

Dissolve 1 tsp. instant coffee in 1 tbsp. milk in each tall glass. Add a scoop of ice cream to each glass. Pour in ginger ale to halfway mark and allow foam to settle; then slowly add the rest of the ginger ale to top up. Serves 2.

COWBOY COFFEE/CAMPFIRE COFFEE

Soldiers in the American Civil War made coffee in large cans which they called a "billies."

Place a small handful of coffee grounds (regular grind) into a can (billy) of cold water (about 1 tbsp. grounds per cup water). Place the can on the fire coals and bring the water to a boil. A froth will form on the top, indicating that the coffee is ready. Throw in 1/4 cup cold water and allow the grounds to settle to the bottom.

When handling the hot can, wear gloves so you don't burn your hands.

Note: In 1878, James Sanborn and Caleb Chase (Chase Sanborn) produced the first ground coffee sealed in tins.

THE COFFEE BOOK

COFFEE-COLA SODA

1 tbsp. cream
Ice cubes
1/2 cup coffee, cooled
1/2 cup carbonated cola drink

Place cream at the bottom of a tall glass. Fill glass with ice cubes. Pour equal amounts of coffee and cola into glass and stir. Serves 1.

COFFEE HAWAIIAN

Near the village of Kona, Hawaii, is the only place in the United States where coffee is grown. Kona coffee is slightly acidic, mellow, and smooth. In this recipe, you taste the sweetness of coconut.

1 cup milk
1/2 cup flaked or shredded coconut
1 tbsp. sugar
1 cup strong hot coffee
2 tsp. shredded coconut

Heat milk. Add 1/2 cup coconut and the sugar. Cover and refrigerate overnight. Strain milk and reheat. Mix hot milk with hot coffee. Pour into cups. Top with toasted coconut.

To toast coconut place 2 tsp. shredded coconut on a piece of foil in oven. Broil until coconut is browned.

Instead of making your own coconut milk, a can of coconut milk may be purchased in specialty stores. Use 1 cup canned coconut milk. Serves 2.

CHILLED HAWAIIAN COFFEE

Make above recipe and refrigerate until chilled. Serve in glasses.

NEW ORLEANS COFFEE BLEND

The French colonists brought their love of dark-roasted coffee to New Orleans. Traditional New Orleans coffee is a very strong, dark-roasted blend of beans with roasted ground chicory root. Make your own.

Mix 70 percent dark-roasted coffee (French or Italian) and 30 percent dark-roasted chicory (it adds thickness and special flavor). Purchase chicory at a specialty store or make your own dark-roasted chicory (see "Coffee Substitutes" section below).

NEW ORLEANS CAFE BRULOT

When the French brought café brûlot from Paris to their colonies (Haiti, Martinique, Louisiana) it became known as café diable. In New Orleans, café brûlot is made in a special silver bowl kept hot over an alcohol flame.

1 stick cinnamon
4 tsp. grated orange peel
2 tsp. grated lemon peel
1/8 tsp. ground nutmeg
10 sugar cubes
1/2 cup plus 2 tbsp. cognac
3 cups freshly brewed espresso coffee

In the blazer pan of a chafing dish (or a double boiler), combine all ingredients except coffee and 2 tbsp. cognac. Heat mixture. In a saucepan, warm 2 tbsp. cognac. Ignite cognac with a match and pour flames over sugar in the chafing dish. Add hot coffee and stir. Serve in demitasse cups. The key to the good taste of café brûlot is the burnt sugar. Serves 6.

VENEZUELA

Venezuelans drink high-grade, fine-ground coffee, made by dripping hot water through a coffee *filtro* (cloth filter) into a container, pot, or carafe. Venezuelans put lots of coffee in the *filtro,* resulting in a strong drink.

Café is drunk with powdered milk. The powdered milk has a high fat content—about 28 percent—which, when reconstituted, makes a thick and creamy milk. The milk is heated in a saucepan to scalding point and poured through the *café filtro* in place of hot water.

In Venezuela, brown sugar is added to make *café con azúcar.* As in Guatemala and El Salvador, the sugar is flaked off of a cone-shaped panela with a knife.

In rural Venezuela the locals rise early (4:30 A.M.) and jump-start their day with a strong black coffee. They leave for work having been shaken awake with the coffee.

When morning chores are taken care of, locals return home to partake in a regular breakfast of *café con leche* with *arepas* (corn bread) or *canilla* (a French-style bread). *Café con leche* is coffee with lots of milk added. Breakfast coffee drinkers, rural or urban, have a custom of dunking *canilla* into their *café con leche*. *Café* is looked upon at breakfast more as a liquid to wash the bread down with. Lunch is Venezuela's largest meal. A *café negro* (black coffee) is usually served.

There isn't a scheduled coffee break for Venezuelan workers like there is in most other Latin American countries. Coffee and pastry are taken at any time of day. The coffee machines in the *panaderías* are constantly pumping demitasses of coffee out for workers in for a quick coffee fix or for those gulping down a breakfast of *café* and pastry en route to work.

An interesting cultural "breadbit" of information to note here is that for years Venezuelans purchased a small bread for their coffee dunking with a coin called a *locha*. When the locha (a small denomination) succumbed to inflation and became obsolete, Venezuelans continued to and still do refer to their favorite bread as the *pan de locha* (bread that costs a *locha*).

Besides the French and the Tunisians, there probably aren't any other people in the world who have as many ways of ordering and referring to *café* as do the Venezuelans. For example, all of the following terms are used:

Café Negro: black *café*.

Café con Leche: *café* with lots of milk (half-milk and half-coffee).

Café con Azúcar: *café* with brown sugar.

Un Marrón: *café* with a small amount of milk. *Marrón* means a brown color or coffee that is brown in color.

Venezuelans indicate the coffee strength desired by ordering *café corto* (short), which means a strong brew, or *café largo* (long), which is slightly more diluted, but is still strong. To make *café largo,* add hot boiling water to a strong brew of coffee, just enough to dilute it a little.

Also, coffee is ordered according to quantity. If a demitasse is desired, one orders a *cafecito*. When ordering in Venezuela, specify the strength and quantity as follows:

Negro: black coffee served in a large cup.

Uno Negro Corto: strong coffee served in a large cup.

Uno Negrito Largo: diluted black coffee served in a demitasse.

Corto: a strong black coffee served in a demitasse.

Marrocito: black coffee served in a small demitasse.

Cafecito con Leche: half-milk and half-coffee served in a demitasse.

VIETNAM

In Vietnam, a dark-roast coffee is brewed in an individual drip pot that sits on top of a glass, slowly dripping coffee into a sweet milk. The coffee and pots are available in Southeast Asian markets, and certainly are a contrast to the espresso method.

CA PHE DA

1-2 tbsp. sweetened condensed milk (room temperature)
2 standard coffee measures (medium-fine grind)
1 cup hot water

Place the milk in the bottom of an 8-oz. glass. Place grounds in the drip pot. Fill with hot water and allow to drip into the glass. It may take up to 15 minutes to drip through, so the brew tends to be lukewarm. Stir milk up from the bottom gently; some of it will remain in the bottom of the cup. Serves 1.

Restaurants use a large earthenware pot heated by wood, with a long, cloth, urn-sized filter bag that hangs down inside the pot. The filter bag is held open at the top by a metal wire. Boiling water is poured into the bag, submerging the coffee grounds. The coffee is steeped and sometimes boiled for 10-15 minutes, producing a very strong brew.

CA PHE DEN (ICED COFFEE)

Follow the above single-cup recipe. Add ice cubes on top of the sweet milk before dripping coffee into the glass.

YEMEN

Coffee first arrived in Yemen from Abyssinia (Ethiopia). Coffee beans are freshly roasted and then pulverized using a mortar and pestle just before use. The coffee grounds and sugar are put into an ibrik:

Helo: 2 tsp. sugar for every cup.
Mazbout: 1 tsp. sugar for every cup.
Murrah: without sugar.
It is made the same way as Arabic or Turkish coffee. Boil twice. Serve in demitasses.

YEMEN GINGER COFFEE

    1 1/2 cups cold water
    3 tbsp. pulverized coffee (dark roast)
    3 tsp. sugar
    1 small piece peeled ginger (grated or pulverized if possible)

Put ingredients into an ibrik. Make Arabic style coffee (see "Turkish Coffee Method" in Brewing Methods chapter). Boil twice. Pour into demitasses. Serves 3.

Traditional After-Dinner Coffees

Hot coffee and liqueurs combine well to make a flavorful partnership. After-dinner coffees are usually prepared with a higher-roast, slightly acidic coffee for a strong taste. The heat of the coffee enhances the flavor of the liqueur. Many countries have made their own unique contribution to the after-dinner coffee.

BASIC AFTER-DINNER COFFEE

Add 1 oz. favorite liquor or liqueur to coffee glass or mug. Fill glass 3/4 full with hot coffee. Top coffee drink with whipped cream. Garnish whipped cream with spices or nut pieces for decoration. Serves 1.

AUSTRIA

KAFFEE MIT SCHLAG

Crème de menthe is a very sweet green liqueur with a strong mint flavor.

2 tsp. chocolate syrup
2 mugs strong coffee (2 coffee measures per cup of water)
2 jiggers crème de menthe
2 scoops whipped cream

Spoon chocolate syrup into 2 cups (1 tsp. per cup) and fill cups 3/4 full with hot coffee. Add 1 jigger of crème de menthe to each cup. Top with whipped cream. Serves 2.

BELGIUM

CAFE BELGE (AFTER-DINNER VERSION)

To a cup of hot mocha coffee, add 1 oz. Elixir d'Anvers. Elixir d'Anvers is a brandy-based liqueur made from herbs and plants in Antwerp, Belgium. It is golden in color, moderately sweet, and very fragrant. Top with whipped cream. Serves 1.

BRAZIL

CAFE QUENTE COM RUM
(HOT SPICED RUM COFFEE)

Top 3/4 cup coffee with whipped cream. Slowly add 1 oz. rum, pouring it over the cream. Garnish whipped cream with cinnamon, nutmeg, or slivered almonds. Serves 1.

CANADIAN WINTER WARMER

Maple liqueur is a very sweet, amber liqueur made from the sap of the maple tree, indigenous to eastern Canada.

1/2 oz. maple liqueur
1/2 oz. brandy
1 cup hot coffee
2 tbsp. whipped cream
2 tbsp. Café Columbo coffee liqueur (optional)

In a mug, add maple liqueur, brandy, and coffee. Top with whipped cream and drizzle Café Columbo liqueur over the top, if desired. Serves 1.

SNOWCAP

Add 1 oz. Bailey's Irish Cream to a cup of cappuccino.

CANADIAN COFFEE

In a mug, combine 1 oz. Amaretto, 1/2 oz. Café Royal coffee liqueur, and 1 cup hot strong coffee. Serves 1.

YUKON JACK COFFEE

Yukon Jack is a bourbon-based whiskey, medium sweet in flavor, that is produced in the Yukon, Canada.

Add 1 1/2 oz. Yukon Jack rye whiskey to a mug of strong hot coffee. This drink is wicked. It will warm you up on a cold winter's night. Serves 1.

COFFEE AT THE LEGION

A vet's recipe.

Spike your coffee with Canadian Club rye whiskey. Try a double.

CARIBBEAN

CAFE CALIPSO

Tía María is a coffee-based liqueur made from the extract of Jamaican Blue Mountain coffee. It has a hint of chocolate flavor. It is lighter and drier than Kahlua. Legend has it that the name comes from Aunt Mary, a servant woman who fled from the country when the British overtook the islands from the Spaniards in the 1600s. She took with her the treasured family recipe to make coffee liqueur, which she continued to use. Eventually, it was rediscovered and once again is produced in the land where it originated.

To 3/4 cup strong dark-roast coffee, add 1 oz. Tía María. Top with whipped cream. Serves 1.

CAFE JAMAICANO

In a tall stemmed glass, place 1 oz. Tía María and 3/4 oz. dark rum. Fill with hot Blue Mountain Blend coffee. Top with whipped cream and sprinkle with nutmeg. Serves 1.

CAFE CON RON

Add 1/2 oz. light rum to a cup of coffee. Top with whipped cream. Serves 1.

CAFE CARIBENO

Jamaica was the first country to produce a pungent dark rum with spirits and molasses. The flavor is buttery with the aroma of molasses. Light rum (white) is a Cuban innovation dating back to the late 1800s. It is lower in proof than dark rum and is aged for a shorter period of time.

To 3/4 cup dark-roast coffee, add 1 oz. dark rum. Sugar to taste. Top with whipped cream. Serves 1.

CAFE DIABLE

2 cups strong coffee
Juice of 1 orange
1 tsp. grated lemon peel
1/2 tsp. cloves
1 cinnamon stick
1 vanilla bean
6 tbsp. cognac

Mix the above ingredients, except cognac, in a pot. Bring to a boil and allow to simmer for 1 minute. Cover pot. Let steep for 5 minutes. Strain into cups. Dribble 3 tbsp. cognac over the back of a spoon onto each drink. Light cognac with a match. Wait until the flame dies before drinking. Serves 2.

CREMAT CUBANO

1 cup light rum
3 tbsp. sugar
1 stick cinnamon
1 strip of orange peel and 1 of lemon
3 cups hot coffee
1 tbsp. coffee beans

Combine rum, sugar, cinnamon, lemon and orange peels in a chafing dish and heat. When heated, light the mixture with a match and flambé for 1 minute. Then douse the mixture with hot coffee, and add coffee beans. Pour into cups immediately. Serves 4.

PRINCE CHARLES COFFEE

Drambuie is a Scotch-based, herb-flavored liqueur with a sharp yet honey-smooth taste. The name comes from a Celtic phrase, dram buid beach, *which means a drink that satisfies. Some say Bonnie Prince Charlie developed the recipe for Drambuie.*

To 3/4 cup coffee, add 1 oz. Drambuie. Serves 1.

ROYAL MINT COFFEE

Royal Mint Chocolate is a clear chocolate-based liqueur developed in England. It has a hint of mint flavor. Chocolate spread to Spain from the Americas in the fifteenth century and later spread through Europe. Chocolate was thought to have aphrodisiac properties and, like peppermint, aided in digestion. Both ingredients were used in love potions and medicinal remedies at one time.

To 3/4 cup coffee, add 1 oz. Royal Mint Chocolate. Serves 1.

ENGLISH COFFEE

Mint Cream Liqueur is a mint-based liqueur either green or white and very sweet. It is believed by its overindulging patrons to aid in digestion; thus it is a welcome follow-up to a full dinner.

Add 1 oz. Mint Cream Liqueur to 1 cup hot coffee. Cover the top with whipped cream. Dribble Mint Cream Liqueur lightly over the whipped cream. Serves 1.

FRANCE

CAFE AU RHUM (COFFEE WITH RUM)

In France, coffee after a meal is traditionally served with liqueurs and cigars.

4 tbsp. white rum
2 tsp. soft dark brown sugar or Demerara
2 cups hot strong black coffee, espresso
2 slices lemon

Using tall glasses, add rum and sugar then pour in coffee. Stir to dissolve sugar. Add a slice of lemon to each cup. Serves 2.

CAFE CHANTILLY

Cognác is an all-grape brandy, amber-colored with a delicate fragrance. It began as brandy from Spain and Italy in the thirteenth century. France began to produce brandy in Armagual, south of Cognac, in the fourteenth century. Today the Champagne region in the Cognac area produces the finest cognac.

2 cups hot black coffee
2 oz. cognac
Cognac crème Chantilly (see France in "Traditional Coffee Recipes" above)

Pour steaming hot coffee into 2 warmed goblets. Add cognac. Then top coffee with cognac crème Chantilly. Serves 2.

CAFE AU MARC DE BOURGOGNE (COFFEE WITH BURGUNDY MARC)

Burgundy Marc is clear or brown-colored liquor with a slightly oily flavor, originating in Burgundy, France. Also known as pomace.

Sugar to taste
4 cups hot coffee
2 oz. Burgundy Marc liqueur
4 tsp. crushed ice

Add sugar to taste to hot coffee in coffeepot. Add Burgundy Marc and stir. Put 1 tsp. crushed ice into each cup. Fill each cup with hot coffee mixture. Serves 4.

CAFE ROYALE (OR CAFE GLORIA)

French-roast coffee
Small sugar cubes
Brandy

Pour coffee into demitasse cups. For each cup, place sugar cube in a spoon and balance it on the cup. Fill spoon with brandy. Ignite brandy on spoon with a match and drop flaming brandy into demitasse.

CAFE NORMANDIE

Normandy was one of the areas in France that initiated the practice of adding a liqueur to coffee. Calvados is a strong and tangy apple brandy produced there.

Hot coffee
1/2 to 1 oz. Calvados brandy
Sugar
Crème Chantilly (optional)

Fill demitasse cup with hot coffee. Pour in Calvados. Sweeten with sugar. Top with crème Chantilly, if desired.

CAFE LIEGEOIS

The French have developed a love for Belgium's Café Liègeois. Their fine cognacs marry well with the sharp taste of the coffee.

Sugar to taste
Cognac to taste
2 cups strong dark-roast coffee
Coffee ice cream or chocolate ice cream
Cocoa powder

Add sugar and cognac to hot coffee. Cool to lukewarm. Pour coffee mixture into tall glasses. Cool glasses of coffee in refrigerator 2 to 3 minutes. Add a scoop or two of ice cream to each glass of coffee. Sprinkle cream lightly with cocoa powder. Serves 2.

CAFE FRERE

Benedictine is an amber-colored, sweet herb liqueur. It is produced in Normandy from the original recipe developed by the Benedictine monks at the Abbey of Fecamp in 1510. The exact formula of twenty-seven herbs remains secret. They are blended with brandy or cognac to produce the cordial Benedictine D.O.M. (Latin acronym meaning to God, most good, most great). Chartreuse is a delicate and distinct herb liqueur with a complex taste produced in Voiron, France. It is made by the Carthusian monks, who have guarded the secret formula of 130 different herbs that was given to them by a captain of French King Henry IV in 1605. Legend holds that it has restorative powers and can prolong one's life.

To 3/4 cup coffee, add 1 oz. Benedictine or Chartreuse. Serves 1.

GERMANY

DEUTSCHER KAFFEE

Kirsch is a fruit-based brandy that is appropriately named by the German word for cherry, signifying its flavor. This delicious brandy is produced in Germany, Switzerland, and France.

Add 1 oz. kirsch into hot coffee. Sugar to taste. Top with whipped cream. Serves 1.

WESTFALIEN KAFFEE

Steinhager is a concentrated liqueur from brandy.

Add 1 oz. Steinhager liqueur to hot black coffee. Top with whipped cream. Serves 1.

ALPEN KAFFEE

Enzian is a spirit distilled in the Alps, made from the yard-long roots of the yellow mountain gentian. It is one of the most aristocratic forms of schnapps.

To hot coffee, add 1 oz. Enzian liqueur. Serves 1.

GREECE

KAFEO OUZO

Ouzo is a clear aniseed-based liqueur with a black-licorice taste.

Add 1 oz. ouzo and 1 oz. coffee liqueur to strong coffee. Top with whipped cream. Serves 1.

KAFEO METAXA

Metaxa is a brandy-based, fruit-flavored liqueur.

Fill a demitasse 2/3 full of strong Greek coffee. Fill a spoon with Metaxa and ignite the liqueur with a match. Drop flaming Metaxa on the spoon into the coffee. Serves 1.

HUNGARY

KAVE PALINKA

Hungary is famous for Barack palinka *(apricot brandy) and* Szilvapalinka *(plum brandy).*

Add 1 oz. of either apricot or plum brandy to a glass of hot coffee. Serves 1.

IRELAND

IRISH COFFEE

Irish whiskey is a strong liquor distilled from a mash of grains (rye, oats, wheat, barley). It has a distinct, full, sweet taste because of the unique method of curing the grains. Crème de cacao is a clear chocolate-flavored liqueur produced in the U.S. that combines chocolate, fruit, and mint.

Add 1 oz. Irish whiskey and 1/2 oz. crème de cacao to strong hot coffee (medium or light roasted). Top with whipped cream and sip coffee through the cream. Serves 1.

IRISH MIST COFFEE

Irish Mist is a Scotch-based liqueur derived from an ancient Irish recipe rediscovered in 1948. It has a rich flavor of herbs and honey.

3/4 cup coffee
1 oz. Irish Mist liqueur
Whipped cream

Combine coffee and Irish Mist. Top with whipped cream. Serves 1.

BAILEY'S IRISH CREAM COFFEE

Bailey's Irish Cream is a rich blend of Irish whiskey and fresh cream that is delivered to a Dublin-based production plant.

Add 1 oz. Bailey's Irish Cream to a warm cup of coffee. Top with whipped cream. Serves 1.

ITALY

Sambuca is traditionally served flaming with three coffee beans in it on the side to accompany one's after-dinner coffee in Italy. Sambuca is a clear licorice-flavored liqueur produced in Italy from the fruit of the elder bush.

CAFFE ALLA MANDORLA

Amaretto di Saronna is a sweet apricot liqueur with a bitter almond flavor. Amaretto is produced worldwide; however, the most popular is Amaretto di Saronna from a small northwestern town in Italy where it originated. The apricot kernel is a close relative to the almond, which is what gives the strong almond flavor, when blended with the apricot flavor from the pulp. A truly romantic tale attributes its invention to a young woman who made the drink for her lover to symbolize her devotion.

Add 1 oz. Amaretto di Saronna to hot coffee. Sugar to taste. Top with whipped cream and sprinkle with slivered almonds. Serves 1.

CAFFE VENEZIANO

Pour 1 oz. brandy into a heated stemmed glass. Fill with dark-roast Italian coffee. Sugar to taste. Top with whipped cream. Serves 1.

CAFFE ALLA STREGA

Strega is an Italian word that means witch. *This liqueur is made from seventy different barks and herbs. Legends hold that a coven of witches used it as a love elixir.*

Add 1 oz. Strega to hot coffee. Sugar to taste. Add a lemon twist. Serves 1.

CAFFE ANISETTE

Anisette liqueur is a sweetened version of anise, a spirit infused with aniseed and wormwood. The licorice-tasting cordial originated in 1755 from a recipe using aniseed and sixteen additional ingredients.

To a demitasse cup of espresso coffee, add 1 oz. anisette liqueur. Serves 1.

CAFFE ROMANO

Galliano is a bright-yellow, honey-sweet herb liqueur made in Rignite, Italy. The name comes from the late nineteenth-century hero who defended a fort in honor of his country. The label on the tall, tapered bottle portrays the fort.

To 1 oz. Galliano and 1 oz. sugar syrup, add hot strong black coffee to 1/2 inch from top of cup and swizzle. Add cream. Serves 1.

NAPOLETANO-FRANGELICO

Frangelico is a hazelnut-flavored liqueur from Italy.

Add 1 oz. Frangelico to a cup of Napoletano-made coffee (see Brewing Methods chapter). Serves 1.

MEXICO

CAFE DE BAJA

Kahlua is a sweet, rich, coffee-flavored liqueur. It has the distinct flavor of Mexican coffee beans. Tequila dates back to the Aztec era. They produced a wine from the mescal plant (a hallucinogenic succulent). The sap is processed and fermented to produce a highly concentrated clear alcohol. White tequila is bottled after one month of aging whereas gold tequila is aged longer. It has a strong herbal flavor and a slightly oily consistency. If you're lucky you will find a bottle with the traditional worm floating at the bottom.

3 tbsp. tequila
2 tbsp. Kahlua (or coffee liqueur)
1 cup hot coffee
Sweetened whipped cream
Sugar to taste

Place tequila, coffee liqueur, and hot coffee into a tall glass. Top with whipped cream. Add sugar as desired. Serves 1.

THE NETHERLANDS

KOFFIE MET ADVOKAAT

Advokaat is a rich, creamy liqueur made from egg yolks, sugar, and spirits.

Pour 1 oz. apricot brandy in stemmed glass. Fill glass to the brim with warm coffee. Top with whipped cream. Dribble 1/2 oz. Advokaat over whipped cream. Serves 1.

RUSSIA

KAPHE BALALAIKA

Vodka is a clear strong spirit produced from starch or sugar (potato, grain, or corn). The name comes from zhizenennia voda, *meaning water of life. Russian production began in the thirteenth century at the Fort of Viataka. Originally vodka was used for medicinal purposes. By the fourteenth century it came into use as a beverage.*

1 cup hot strong black coffee
4 tsp. vodka
2 tsp. brown sugar
4 tsp. heavy cream

Combine coffee, vodka, and sugar in a glass. Stir. Pour cream slowly over the back of a rounded spoon held close to the top of the coffee, so the cream dribbles down in a layer on top of the coffee. Serve at once. In Russia coffee is served in glasses set in filigreed metal glass holders with handles. Serves 1.

SCANDINAVIA

SCANDINAVIAN KAFFE

Aquavit is a clear cordial, distilled from grain or potatoes, with a distinctive caraway taste and a hint of cardamom and anise. For several hundred years it has been known as the national drink of Denmark, which is still the center for its production.

To basic hot coffee recipe, add 1 oz. Aquavit. Serves 1.

SWEDISH GLOGG

A hot spicy coffee with light rum, commonly served during festive occasions.

1 tbsp. butter
1/2 cup brown sugar
1/8 tsp. ground ginger
1/8 tsp. ground cloves
1/8 tsp. ground allspice
1/8 tsp. ground nutmeg
1/4 cup heavy cream
1/4 cup light rum
3 cups strong hot coffee

Cream butter, sugar, and spices together. Put 1 tsp. mixture into each cup. Add 1 tbsp. each of cream and rum to each cup. Pour in hot coffee and serve. Serves 4.

SCOTLAND

SCOTS COFFEE

Scotch whiskey comes in a variety of special grain and malt blends (more than two thousand varieties in Scotland), although single-malt scotches are preferred by true scotch drinkers. The pioneers of Scotch whiskey were distilling in the late 1800s. A strong hot coffee complements the subtle flavors of the drink.

Add 1 oz. Scotch whiskey to 3/4 cup hot coffee. Add cream to taste. Serves 1.

GAELIC COFFEE

Glen Mist liqueur is a Scotch-based liqueur, one of the best known of the Royal Chocolate liqueurs. It is a delicious, honey-smooth, yet tangy liqueur and blends well with after-dinner coffee.

To 3/4 cup coffee, add 1 oz. Glen Mist liqueur. Serves 1.

CAFE ESPAGNOL

2/3 oz. brandy
1/3 oz. coffee liqueur
Hot coffee

Combine in snifter. Rim glass with sugar. Top with whipped cream and a maraschino cherry. Serves 1.

CAFE DE CIRUELAS (PRUNE CAFE)

This coffee with brandy and prunes drink was developed in the Basque region of Spain (very medicinal).

2 cups strong freshly brewed coffee
1 cup Spanish brandy
2 tbsp. brown sugar
6-8 dried prunes
1/2 cup heavy cream, partially whipped

Combine hot coffee, brandy, and sugar in a coffeepot. Drop 2 prunes into each glass and pour in coffee mixture. Lay the cream on top of each drink by slowly dribbling it over the back of a spoon. Serves 3-4.

MONTE CRISTO

Grand Marnier is an orange-flavored cordial still made by the Lapostalle family since the late 1800s by blending Haitian oranges with fine French cognac.

Sugar
2/3 oz. Grand Marnier
Hot coffee
Whipped cream
1/3 oz. coffee liqueur

Rim glass with sugar. Combine Grand Marnier and coffee in glass. Top with whipped cream. Drizzle coffee liqueur over whipped cream. Serves 1.

THAILAND

GHA FAA SIAM

This is a very sweet after-dinner drink made with Mekong. Mekong is a rice spirit with a close affinity to whiskey, and is the national liquor of Thailand.

Put 1 1/2 oz. Mekong in a long-stemmed glass. Heat the alcohol over a Bunsen-type flame and then light the alcohol with a match. While the alcohol is flaming in the glass, take 1 tbsp. brown sugar and dip into the flame. Spread the melting brown sugar in a line around the inside center of the glass. When the sugar is spread around the glass, put the flame out by filling the glass 3/4 full with hot strong coffee (Indonesian bean). Drop 4 whipped cream balls into the coffee. Serves 1.

Whipped cream balls: To make, start by holding a spoon in each hand. Pass a teaspoonful of whipped cream (beaten stiff with lots of sugar added) back and forth, molding it into a ball with the spoons.

UNITED STATES

B-52 COFFEE

This is a "knockout" drink, named after the American B-52 bomber airplane.

1/3 oz. Irish cream
1/3 oz. coffee liqueur
1/3 oz. Grand Marnier
Hot coffee

Combine ingredients in a snifter, or layer the liqueurs in a small shooter glass to accompany a cup of hot coffee. Top with whipped cream. Garnish with cherry. Serves 1.

MARDI GRAS COFFEE

Southern Comfort is a well-guarded family secret of a bourbon-based whiskey, flavored with peach extracts and citrus essence. It has a distinctive, strong, sweet taste. It was first made in 1875, in New Orleans, known as Cuff and Buttons (white tie and tails) and later was dubbed Southern Comfort by a St. Louis bartender.

Prepare New Orleans-style coffee with chicory, adding 1/2 tsp. cinnamon and 1/4 tsp. allspice into the coffee grounds before brewing. Add 1 1/2 oz. Southern Comfort and 1/2 oz. apricot brandy to hot coffee and pour in cups. Top with whipped cream. Garnish with grated orange peel. Serves 2-4.

SOUTHERN SLUDGE

1 oz. Jack Daniels
1/2 oz. Amaretto
Dark strong coffee

Combine all ingredients; stir. Serve with a topping of whipped cream if desired. Serves 1.

Iced Coffees

Coffee makes a refreshing drink either chilled and served over ice or partially frozen. Iced coffees can be prepared using ground coffee, instant coffee, or coffee syrup.

1. With Ground Coffee: Make double-strength coffee by using 4 level tbsp. coffee to each cup water. (Coffee is made double-strength coffee so when the ice melts the coffee won't be too watery.) Pour into a pitcher (with lid) and refrigerate until cool. Serve over ice.

Or utilize that leftover coffee that has cooled to room temperature to make coffee ice cubes. Add these to hot coffee to make iced coffee.

2. With Instant Coffee: Mix 3 heaping tbsp. instant coffee granules and 2 rounded tbsp. powdered sugar in a bowl. Add 5 cups boiling water to dissolve granules and sugar. Whisk 2 1/2 cups cold milk into the coffee mixture. Refrigerate in a pitcher (with lid) for 2 hours. Serve over ice in a tall glass.

3. **With Coffee Syrup:** To make coffee syrup:

> 3/4 cup granulated sugar
> 1 1/4 cups boiling water
> 4 heaping tbsp. instant coffee

Heat the sugar and water in a saucepan and stir until sugar is dissolved. Stir in the instant coffee. Refrigerate in a pitcher with lid until cool.

Pour 1/2 oz. to 1 oz. coffee syrup into a glass. Add 2 ice cubes and fill glass with cold water. Add cream or milk if desired. Or substitute chilled milk for cold water if a milkier beverage is preferred.

BRANDIED COFFEE ICE

> **1 pot coffee (8 cups)**
> **2 jiggers or 3 oz. brandy**
> **Sugar to taste**

Pour into ice-cube trays. For a cool drink, place two cubes in a cup and pour hot coffee over.

LIQUEUR ICES

Combine your favorite liqueur to taste with a pot of double-strength coffee. Freeze mixture in ice-cube trays. Serve in iced coffees, cocktails, and frappes, where crushed ice is called for.

KAHLUA COFFEE ICE

> **Double-strength coffee or espresso**
> **Kahlua**
> **Vanilla extract**

Combine and freeze in trays. Add to any cocktail calling for coffee liqueur.

ITALIAN ICE COCKTAIL

Make ice cubes with espresso coffee. Crush coffee ice and fill cocktail glass with it. Pour 1 oz. Galliano or any other preferred liqueur over coffee ice.

COFFEE COOLER

Pour cold coffee into ice-cube trays and freeze. When frozen, blend ice cubes into ice shavings or crushed ice and place in a cocktail glass. Pour your favorite liqueur over top.

BANANA COOLER

Place in your blender 1 cup cold coffee, 1/2 cup brandy, and 1 ripe banana. Blend until thick and creamy. Serve in a tall glass, "straight up" or over ice. Serves 1.

COFFEE TROPICALE

Crushed ice
4 tsp. sugar
1 1/2 cups strong cold coffee

Fill the container of an electric blender half-full with crushed ice. Add sugar and coffee. Cover and blend on high speed for about 1 minute, or until thick and creamy. Pour into tall chilled glasses. Serves 4.

CARNIVAL COFFEE

1 cup milk
1/2 cup cold strong coffee
1/2 cup dark rum
1/4 cup crushed ice
1 ripe banana
Ground nutmeg

Blend the first 5 ingredients until thick and creamy. Pour into tall glasses. Sprinkle each drink with ground nutmeg. Serves 2.

AN ESPRESSO MILK SHAKE

Fill a blender with as much ice cream as your heart desires (suggest vanilla, mocha, spumoni). Throw in 1 tbsp. espresso coffee powder (finely ground). Remember to add in a couple cups of milk. Blend espresso powder, ice cream, and milk until thick and creamy. Indulge! Serves 4-6.

BALINESE COFFEE

1 cup cold coffee
1 scoop vanilla ice cream

Pour coffee over ice in a tall glass. Top with ice cream. Serve with a straw and long-handled spoon.

GRANITA DI CAFFE CON PANNO

A combination of a flavor and ice, called granite or semisoft ice, is popular in Italy during the summer months. One of the favorites is flavored with espresso coffee.

3/4 cup sugar
2 cups water
1/2 cup strong Italian espresso
1 cup heavy cream, whipped with sugar until stiff

This recipe is easy to make if you have a blender. The coffee should be strong (double strength) as coffee taste is diminished when cold. Combine sugar and water in saucepan. Bring to a boil and simmer until the sugar dissolves. Remove from the heat and add espresso. Cool mixture, transfer it to ice-cube trays (grids removed), and freeze. Remove ice from trays and blend, breaking up until ice is almost at "crushed" stage. Place in freezer again for 1 hour. Transfer into the refrigerator to soften before serving. Granita should look "slushy."

Serve in tall glasses or glass bowls, putting in sweetened whipped cream first, then coffee ice, and then more whipped cream. A fancy dessert granita for more formal occasions can be created by dribbling an Italian liqueur over the inside and top layers of whipped cream. Serves 4.

Make Your Own Coffee-Flavored Liqueurs

Add coffee liqueurs to after-dinner coffees in the place of store-bought liqueurs. One ounce of homemade coffee liqueur added to a cup of hot black coffee is nice. Top with whipped cream.

COFFEE LIQUEUR #1

6 tbsp. freshly ground coffee
1 tsp. vanilla extract
4 cups vodka
Sugar syrup (see below)

In a sterilized jar, put freshly ground coffee (use Mexican or your favorite coffee bean), vanilla extract, and vodka. Cover jar tightly. Cover with brown paper and label with date. Store in a warm cupboard for 2 weeks. Shake jar once a day for the first 4 days and once a week thereafter. After 2 weeks filter coffee through cheesecloth, if needed. Add sugar syrup to taste.

Sugar syrup: In a saucepan, put 1/2 cup water and 1 cup sugar. Heat and stir until sugar dissolves and the syrup is clear. Cool. Add to the coffee-vodka to your preference for sweetness. Bottle liqueur in sterilized dark-colored bottles with lids tightly sealed. Recipe may be doubled.

COFFEE LIQUEUR #2

1 1/2 cups vodka
1 cup sugar
1 cup water
1 cup Demerara sugar
1 tsp. vanilla
5 tbsp. freeze-dried coffee

Mix the ingredients in a 2-qt. jar. Put lid on jar and shake. Place in cupboard at room temperature for 2 weeks. Store liqueur in a dark-colored bottle.

ORANGE COFFEE LIQUEUR

1 1/2 cups white sugar
1 cup packed brown sugar
2 cups water
1/3 cup instant coffee
2 cups brandy
2 cups vodka
1/2 skin of orange (no white)
1 vanilla bean

Combine sugar, brown sugar, and water in saucepan. Bring to a boil and simmer uncovered for 10 minutes, stirring occasionally. Stir in coffee to dissolve. Pour coffee mixture, brandy, and vodka into a 2-qt. sterilized glass jar. Add orange skin and vanilla bean. Seal well with a lid. Place in a dark cupboard and allow to stand at room temperature for the day, shaking the jar occasionally.

HOMEMADE TIA MARIA

3 1/2 cups sugar
2 1/4 cups water
4 1/2 tbsp. good quality instant freeze-dried coffee (suggest Taster's Choice)
26 oz. vodka

Bring sugar, water, and coffee grounds to rolling boil; turn to simmer for 12 minutes. Cool to room temperature. Add vodka to mixture. Store in large clean jars with lids on for a few hours.

MOCHA CREAM LIQUEUR

This drink goes down very smoothly but watch out . . . you will be feeling the effects of it shortly after indulging.

6 oz. whipping cream
1 cup sweetened condensed milk (thick)
3 eggs, beaten
4 tbsp. or more good quality chocolate syrup
2 tsp. instant coffee powder or to taste
1 1/2 cups Irish whiskey

Blend all ingredients except whiskey just until combined. Then blend in good quality whiskey (suggest Bushmills). Serve and slurp. This liqueur recipe is one that you can whip up minutes before your guests arrive. Or you can bottle this liqueur and take it along to a Yuletide potluck. Serves 4.

Coffee Cocktails

Cold black coffees or coffee-flavored liqueurs (Kahlua, Tía María, or Aloha) marry well with spirits and ice.

CAFE ALEXANDRE

2 tbsp. crème de cacao
2 tbsp. brandy
2 tbsp. whipped cream
2 tbsp. strong cold coffee
Sugar to taste
Crushed ice
Slivered chocolate

Blend liquors, whipped cream, coffee, and sugar together. Pour over crushed ice. Top with slivered chocolate. Serves 1.

CAFE FRAPPE

2 oz. strong cold coffee
2 oz. your favorite liqueur
Shaved ice

Add coffee and liqueur to shaved ice in a shaker. Shake well and pour into a frappé glass. Serves 1.

KAFEO GRECO

Triple Sec is a clear orange-flavored liqueur. Cointreau is a clear orange-flavored premium French brandy.

1/3 cup Metaxa
1/3 cup Triple Sec or Cointreau
1/3 cup cold black coffee
Ice

Shake ingredients well and strain into a cocktail glass. Serves 3.

The following recipes are American versions.

BLACK RUSSIAN

1 oz. vodka
1/2 oz. coffee liqueur
Ice

Pour liquids over ice into an old-fashioned glass. Serves 1.

WHITE RUSSIAN

1 oz. vodka
1/2 oz. coffee liqueur
Cream to fill
Ice

Pour liquids over ice into an old-fashioned glass. Serves 1.

MOSCOW MIST

2 oz. vodka
1 tsp. instant coffee powder
1 tsp. lemon juice
1 cup shaved ice
Sugar to taste

Mix all ingredients in a blender at high speed for 30-60 seconds. Serves 1.

UNITED STATES

ICED KONA COFFEE

Make coffee and sugar to taste. Chill. Fill a tall glass or mug with cracked ice and pour coffee over it. Add 1 oz. Kahlua liqueur. Top with whipped cream.

DIRTY MOTHER

1/2 oz. tequila
1/2 oz. coffee liqueur
Cream to fill
Ice cubes
Cherry

Pour liquids over ice cubes. Garnish with cherry.

BARTENDER'S ROOT BEER

Liquore d'Oro is a yellow liqueur with a vanilla and licorice taste.

1/2 oz. Liquore d'Oro
1/2 oz. coffee liqueur
Soda water to fill
Dash of cola
Ice cubes
Orange slice and cherry

Pour liquids over ice cubes in a tall glass. Garnish with orange and cherry.

Instant Coffees

In 1906, instant coffees were produced, which made coffee preparation extremely easy. There are many brands that use low-grade coffees which are reflected in the brew they produce. If you are going to use an instant coffee, choose a good brand of freeze-dried granules. A single (light) cream will enhance the flavor better than will milk. Also, prepare in a coffee butler (heatproof container). Instant coffees are particularly popular in countries that do not produce coffee or cannot afford to import coffee beans.

MOCHA JAVA

1 tbsp. instant coffee
2 tbsp. instant chocolate mix
2 oz. milk
2 oz. water

Place coffee and chocolate in a 5-oz. cup. In a saucepan, heat milk and water. Add to cup.

SPICY MOCHA JAVA

To above Mocha Java recipe, add a dash of cinnamon and a dash of nutmeg.

MOCHA MIX

1/2 cup sugar
1 tsp. ground nutmeg
1/4 cup freeze-dried coffee
1/2 tsp. ground cinnamon
1/4 cup cocoa

To make mix place all ingredients in blender container. Cover and blend on high speed for 15 seconds. Stir. Cover and blend until completely mixed, about 15 seconds. Store in tightly covered container. Makes about 1 cup.

For each serving place 2 to 3 tsp. mix in cup. Fill with boiling water. Stir. Top with whipped topping if desired.

ORANGE MOCHA COFFEE

To above recipe, add 1 tbsp. orange drink crystals (or powdered orange juice) or dried orange rind.

Coffee Substitutes

Throughout history, there have been times when coffee was not available to coffee drinkers. These times were usually associated with wars, famines, depressions, and eras of colonization. As mankind sought to approximate the taste of coffee in other ways, many other plants have been roasted and ground, and prepared in decoctions. Today, tea and coffee substitutes are continuing to gain popularity.

CHICORY COFFEE (KAFFEE ERSATZ)

It is believed that roasted ground chicory roots were first used as a coffee substitute in 1770 in Germany. *Kaffee Ersatz* was much in use during World War I and II, when coffee was hard to come by and not affordable. Chicory's ability to blend well with coffee, tea leaves, or herbs has long been known. It also makes a good coffee stretcher and it lends unique qualities to coffee, adding a darker color and longer-lasting flavor. Chicory is also known as coffeeweed and wild endive.

To prepare your own, dig up the long roots of the chicory plant in the summer. Clean the roots well and chop in 1/2-inch lengths. Place chicory on a baking sheet and roast in the oven at 250 degrees. Chicory is adequately roasted when it is brown and very dry. Grind dry chicory the same way you would grind roasted coffee beans. Store in an airtight container.

To substitute chicory grounds for coffee, increase the amount you would use for coffee grounds. Chicory powder may be percolated or used in a drip coffee maker. Use 1 tbsp. chicory powder for every 2 tsp. coffee grounds normally used.

GRAIN COFFEE

In North America the staple ersatz coffee after World War I and World War II was made from grains (barley, rye, or wheat). To make a grain coffee, roast grains in oven at about 250 degrees until dark brown in color. Mix with chicory grounds or make a grain coffee by using 1 tsp. grain grounds to 1 cup boiling water. Sweeten with honey.

DANDELION ROOT COFFEE

In its dried and roasted form, dandelion is considered a good coffee substitute. Pull the dandelions at the end of summer. Separate and clean the roots. Roast the dandelion roots in the oven (250 degrees) until the roots are brittle. Store dried roots in an airtight container. When ready for use, grind the roots in a coffee grinder and make the same as you would drip coffee. Dandelion coffee may be made using the drip coffee method or percolation. Dandelion grounds may be mixed with coffee grounds for a coffee blend. Sweeten to taste.

JUNIPER BERRY COFFEE

Juniper berries *(Juniperus communis)* can be roasted to make a sweet coffee substitute. Collect the ripe berries in late fall. Dry and store them. Roast the berries in an oven at 250 degrees until dark brown. Grind to a powder. Use the same way as you would coffee grounds to prepare coffee (approximately 1 tbsp. Juniper Berry Coffee Powder to 1 cup boiling water). Juniper berries are used as a gin and liqueur flavoring. *Caution:* Do not use during pregnancy or with kidney inflammation.

Contemporary Coffee Ideas

MORE RECIPES

MOCHA CREAM COFFEE

1/2 cup medium-grind coffee
4 1/2 cups cold water
3 tbsp. chocolate syrup
1/2 cup crème de cacao
Sweetened whipped cream
Shaved chocolate

Brew the coffee and water in a drip coffee maker. Pour into coffee cups. Add chocolate syrup and crème de cacao to the cups. Top with whipped cream and garnish with shaved chocolate. Serves 4.

ALMOND COFFEE

1 tbsp. chocolate syrup
1 tbsp. almond syrup
1 cup espresso coffee
Steamed milk

Combine syrups in a glass and fill 3/4 full with espresso coffee. Add steamed milk to fill glass and spoon foam on top. Serves 1.

Almond syrup: Called Orgeat by Torani, it may be purchased at specialty stores. Orgeat contains almonds and cane sugar.

HOT CHOCOLATE ALMOND ESPRESSO

1 tbsp. chocolate syrup
1 tbsp. almond syrup
1/2 cup espresso coffee
1/2 cup hot chocolate
Whipped cream
Grated chocolate

Combine syrups in a cup. Fill cup to one-half mark with coffee. Add hot chocolate to fill cup. Top with whipped cream and garnish with grated chocolate.

CHOCOLATE ALMOND COFFEE

1/2 cup medium-grind coffee (Colombian)
4 tsp. almonds, coarsely ground
1 tbsp. cocoa
1/4 tsp. ground nutmeg
1/2 tsp. almond extract
4 1/2 cups boiling water

Combine coffee, almond grounds, cocoa, and nutmeg. Pour almond extract over coffee mixture in the filter basket. Add boiling water to the coffee maker and brew as per instructions. Pour into cups and add sugar and cream as desired. Serves 4.

SPECIAL SPICED COFFEE

1/2 cup coffee (medium grind)
1/2 tsp. ground cardamom
1/2 tsp. almond extract
1/2 tsp. vanilla extract
4 1/2 cups water

Place coffee grounds in a filter basket. Sprinkle with cardamom. Pour almond and vanilla extract over the coffee mixture. Add water to the coffee maker and brew. Serve in cups. Add sugar and cream to taste. Serves 4.

CINNAMON COFFEE

4 tbsp. coffee grounds (fine grind)
1 tbsp. cinnamon powder
Coffeepot of water
Demerara sugar
Cream

Place coffee grounds in coffee filter basket of drip coffee maker. Sprinkle cinnamon over the grounds. Add water to coffee maker and brew, as per coffee maker instructions. Serve in mugs. Add Demerara sugar and cream to taste. Serves 4.

COFFEE EGGNOG

3 eggs, separated
1 cup half and half cream
1 cup milk
1/4 cup sugar
1/2 cup brandy
1 cup light rum
2 cups strong coffee
Pinch of salt
1/2 cup heavy cream, whipped
Ground nutmeg

Beat egg yolks until thick and lemon colored. Blend in half and half, milk, sugar, brandy, rum, coffee, and salt. Beat egg whites until stiff. Fold the egg whites into the coffee mixture. Pour into glasses. Top with a dollop of whipped cream. Sprinkle with nutmeg. Serves 6.

KAHLUA NOG (PARTY BLEND)

Eggnog is an American invention dating back to the 1700s. Traditionally eggnog was characterized by the ingredients eggs, milk, and sugar. Later, brandy, rum, or wine was added to it. Nowadays, a variety of spirits are added to the basic egg-milk-sugar mixture, creating new tastes. It is customary in the U.S.A. and Canada to serve eggnog during the Yuletide.

1 cup milk or 1/2 cup milk and 1/2 cup cream
2 tsp. instant coffee
3 large eggs
3 oz. whiskey or brandy (optional)
2 oz. Kahlua
Sugar to taste (optional)

Blend ingredients until mixture is thick and bubbly. Serve over cracked ice. Serves 2. Recipe may be doubled or tripled when making drinks for a social gathering.

Note: Kahlua Nog contains almost as much alcohol as it does milk. If you've been blending pitchers of this festive drink all evening for your guests, be sure to arrange for their safe transportation home.

CHILLED KONA COFFEE

4 standard coffee measures of medium-grind Kona coffee
4 1/2 cups cold water
2 cups pineapple juice, chilled
1 qt. ice cream, softened

Brew the coffee and water in a drip coffee maker. Chill coffee in refrigerator. Combine chilled coffee, pineapple juice, and ice cream. Beat at a low speed with electric mixer or in blender until smooth and frothy. Pour into tall glasses. Serves 6.

SHERRY SPIKE

To hot coffee, add 1/2 oz. Kahlua, 1/2 oz. Amaretto, and a dash of sherry. Serves 1.

HOT SHOTS

To 1 oz. of your favorite liqueur, add 1/2 oz. hot coffee to heat up your liqueur. Serves 1.

CAFE PYRAMID

To hot coffee, add 3/4 oz. brandy, 1/2 oz. Galliano, and 1/4 oz. Cointreau. Top with whipped cream. Serves 1.

KAHLUA AND CREAM POUSSE-CAFE

Layering liquids can be a fun and decorative way to serve coffee drinks to guests. Each liquid has its own weight and when making a layered drink, the lightest will float on top of the heaviest. To make a Kahlua and Cream Pousse-Café, layer Kahlua and heavy cream alternately in a liqueur glass by placing a spoon against the inside of the glass, just above the last layer of liquid. Trickle Kahlua and cream over the back of the spoon into layers as slowly as possible. If you want to become an expert at making pousse-cafés, you can purchase a hydrometer, which measures the weights of liquids. Measure the weights of your favorite liquors and layer them into glasses from the heaviest to the lightest.

STEAMED COFFEE-MILK

Steam a cup of milk with your cappuccino maker. When the milk is steamed, stir in 3/4 tsp. espresso coffee powder to give the milk a coffee taste.

MOLASSES MILK COFFEE

Add 1 tbsp. Barbados or Blackstrap unsulphured molasses into 1/2-3/4 cup milk or 1/4 cup milk and 1/4 cup cream. Mix. Serve molasses milk in a cream pitcher. Let guests add preferred amount to coffee.

MAPLE MILK COFFEE

Add 1 tbsp. maple syrup to 1/2 cup milk or cream or mixture. Stir. Add desired amount of maple milk to coffee.

COFFEE WITH ANGOSTURA BITTERS

Angostura bitters is an aromatic preparation made from the gentian root. The original recipes for it were created in 1924 by Dr. J. G. B. Siegert & Sons Ltd. The yellow gentian is the most bitter-tasting plant known to man. For 2,000 years it has been used in medicines and tonics to aid in gastrointestinal difficulties. It is said to help increase appetites.

Add a few drops of angostura bitters to a sweet coffee. Or to 3/4 cup coffee, add enough cream to make a very creamy, light coffee. Then add 1-2 tbsp. chocolate syrup to coffee. Touch off with a few dashes of bitters to taste. When you become addicted to this drink, you'll find yourself adding more and more drops of these delicious tasting bitters—truly a delicious recipe.

CHRISTY'S DECAF

A friend of one of the authors puts together this decaffeinated coffee blend. Christy removes one-quarter of the coffee grounds from a can of Sanka Decaffeinated Coffee and replaces it with Grand-Marnier-flavored coffee grounds. The flavored grounds take away the slight bitter taste of the Sanka. A very mellow blend!

COFFEE LIQUEUR FARE

Kahlua has been used as the coffee liqueur in the following recipes. Instead of Kahlua, you could substitute with your favorite commercial liqueur (Tía María, Café Royal, Café Columbo) or your own homemade coffee liqueur.

These recipes are meant to follow a 2:1 ratio of the first liquor to the second liquor. For example, for each drink add 1 1/2 oz. of the first liquor and 3/4 oz. of the second liquor (or 1 oz. of the first and 1/2 oz. of the second) to the glass unless otherwise specified. In our opinion, all drinks benefit from the addition of cream or a lightly beaten egg, but this inclusion is, of course, the drinker's choice.

Experiment by combining coffee liqueur with your own favorite liquor and create your own coffee drink.

A Belligerent Sailor: dark rum, Kahlua.
A Noisy Scot: Glayva, Kahlua.
A Dandy Brandy: brandy, Kahlua.
Café Cerise: cherry brandy, Kahlua.
Sherry Daredevil: 1 oz. sherry, 1 oz. Kahlua (suggest cream).

Tequila Sunrise: Kahlua, tequila.

Tequila Sunset: tequila, Kahlua.

Un Grand Café: Kahlua, Grand Marnier, 1 tbsp. orange juice optional (suggest cream).

Holy Hell: Kahlua, Benedictine D.O.M. (suggest cream).

Brown Cow: 1 oz. Kahlua, fill rest of glass with milk, cream, or half and half. Serve in short or tall glasses, straight or over ice.

Café Cacao: Kahlua, crème de cacao, cream.

Mint Coffee: Kahlua, white crème de menthe.

Sweet Mocha Mint: equal amounts Kahlua, white crème de cacao, and white crème de menthe.

To create frappés with these drinks, omit the cream or beaten egg and serve "straight" up or over crushed ice in chilled frappé glasses.

To create "Liquor Mists," serve drinks in old-fashioned glasses over cracked ice or ice cubes.

A COFFEE BAR

As many ideas start in restaurants and eventually reach the home, bring the coffee bar home! A coffee bar adds a special finale to any dinner party or can also stand alone as the focal point for a get-together. It takes a minimal amount of preparation for maximum enjoyment. Guests can mix their own special brew with a little guidance.

Prepare either an Italian espresso or a blend of 30 percent French and 70 percent Colombian in a drip pot. Allow at least 2 servings of coffee per guest. Set out either demitasses or regular cups for each person.

Prepare the following toppings:

Whipped cream: whip up about 1/8 cup unwhipped cream, sweetened lightly with sugar, for each guest. Flavor with vanilla as desired.

Sugar: granulated sugar in a bowl.

Cream: a small pitcher of cream.

Semisweet chocolate: grate up approximately 1 tbsp. per guest. Serve in a bowl.

Spices: provide cinnamon sticks and shakers with ground cinnamon and ground nutmeg.

Seasonings: provide a bowl with grated orange peel, a shaker with powdered chocolate, a bowl with almond slivers.

Liqueurs and spirits: decide on which recipes you want to offer and set out decanters of Frangelico, crème de menthe, peppermint schnapps, crème de cacao, Sambuca, coconut liqueur, Kahlua, cognac. Write out recipe cards for the following, or choose recipes from the "Traditional After-Dinner Coffees" section, and make the cards available to guests at the coffee bar.

AFTER EIGHT

Coffee, 1 oz. Kahlua, 1/2 oz. crème de menthe, top with whipped cream, sprinkle with nutmeg.

VIENNESE COFFEE

Cappuccino, 1 oz. Sambuca, sprinkle with cinnamon, or chocolate shavings and grated orange peel.

CARIBBEAN COFFEE

Coffee, 1 oz. coconut liqueur, top with whipped cream, garnish with almonds.

BANANANA

Coffee, crème de bananes, cream to fill.

SCHNAPPS DELIGHT

Espresso coffee, peppermint schnapps, crème de cacao.

CAFE DE PARIS

Coffee, 1 1/2 oz. cognac, cream.

CAFE MEXICANO (NONALCOHOLIC)

Coffee, cinnamon stick, top with whipped cream, sprinkle with grated chocolate.

GOOD NIGHT

Coffee, 1 oz. Frangelico, 1 oz. Bailey's Irish Cream, top with whipped cream.

BONNE NUIT

Espresso coffee, 1 oz. Frangelico, 1 oz. crème de cacao, top with whipped cream.

A NIGHTCAP

1/2 cup coffee, 1 1/2 oz. Frangelico, 1/2 cup steamed or heated milk.

Adiós. . . . Enjoy.

The Word *Coffee*
Around the World

Café	French-speaking countries: Algeria, Belgium, France, Gambia, Haiti, Martinique
Café	Portuguese-speaking countries: Brazil, Macao, Portugal
Café	Spanish-speaking countries: Colombia, Costa Rica, Cuba, Dominican Republic, El Salvador, Guatemala, Honduras, Jamaica, Mexico, Peru, Spain, Venezuela
Cafea	Rumania
Caffa	Israel
Caffe	Italy
Cā phê	Vietnam
Coffee	Australia, Britain, Canada, Ireland, New Zealand, South Africa, U.S.A.
Coffi	Wales
Gabi	Taiwan
Gafe	Kampuchea (Cambodia)
Gahaveh (Ghahve)	Iran
Gahwah (Gahweh)	Ethiopia
Gha faa	Thailand
Gka-pi	Burma
Gkoubpih	Taiwan (Hokkien dialect)
Kaafee (Kaafii)	India (Hindu)
Kaapi	Sri Lanka (Tamil)
Kafa	Serbia
Kafe	Albania

163

Kafei	China (Mandarin)
Kafeo	Greece
Kaffe	Denmark, Norway, Sweden
Kaffee	Austria, Germany, Switzerland
Kaffi	Iceland
Kahve	Turkey
Kahvi	Finland
Kahwa	Egypt, Tunisia
Kape	Philippines (Tagalog)
Kaphe	Russia
Kapi	Ukraine
Kava	Czech, Slovakia
Kava	Croatia, Serbia
Kawa	Poland
Kawah	Arabia
Kawah	Tanzania
Khahue	Armenia
Kofe	Samoa
Koffie	The Netherlands
Kofi	Tonga
Kohii	Japan
Kophi	Bangladesh, Bengal Province
Kopi	India (Sinhalese)
Kopi	Indonesia (Malay), Korea, Malaysia (Malay), Pidgin (Papua New Guinea)
Kovi	Fiji
Qahwah	Libya, Morocco
Soorj	Armenia
Taofe	Tahiti

THE COFFEE BOOK

The Last Drop
from the Authors

The authors wish to acknowledge that there are countries in the world from which we have yet to obtain recipes. . . . We have not forgotten about you. It is our hope that with continued printing of this book, we will be able to include the coffee drink customs of these countries within future editions.

To our readers, if there are any of you who would like to contribute to this book, enabling our fellow coffee drinkers to share in another cultural version of the coffee drink, we would appreciate it if you would contact us through Pelican Publishing Company, c/o *The Coffee Book*. Until then, it has been a pleasure serving you. . . .

Sincerely, Dawn Campbell and Janet Smith

Measurements

Abbreviations

STANDARD

tsp. = teaspoon
tbsp. = tablespoon
c. = cup
oz. = ounce
qt. = quart

METRIC

ml = milliliter
l = liter
g = gram
kg = kilogram

Standard-Metric Approximations

1/8 tsp. = .6 ml
1/4 tsp. = 1.2 ml
1/2 tsp. = 2.5 ml
1 tsp. = 5 ml
1 tbsp. = 15 ml
2 tbsp. = 1 standard coffee measure
4 tbsp. = 1/4 c. = 60 ml
8 tbsp. = 1/2 c. = 118 ml
16 tbsp. = 1 c. = 236 ml
2 cups = 473 ml
1 oz. = 2 tbsp.
1 1/2 oz. = 1 jigger

Glossary

ambergris: an amber waxy substance found floating in or on the shores of tropical waters, believed to originate in the intestine of the sperm whale. Used primarily in perfumes as a fixative.

billy: coffeepot for open/campfire. A billy is made from a large can with a wire handle attached to two places on the rim.

caffeine: an odorless, white alkaloid that has stimulative properties to the central nervous system. Caffeine is naturally found in coffee beans, tea leaves, and cocoa beans.

chantilly: sweetened whipped cream.

cherries: the ripe fruit of the coffee tree, which contains the coffee seeds (beans).

Demerara: a partially refined, coarse, beige-toned crystal containing the molasses portion of the sugar.

demitasse: small three- or four-ounce cup usually without a handle. Available in coffee specialty shops.

essence: a concentrated extract derived from the coffee bean.

faux pas: a mistake or error; a socially non-acceptable action.

flambé: heated brandy or liquor that is flamed for dramatic effect for the serving of meats, desserts, and coffees.

flavored coffee: roasted coffee that has been dusted with powders or sprayed with oils to add flavor.

liquefy: to blend ingredients until a smooth consistency is achieved.

liqueur: a spirit beverage made from the essences of herbs, spices, fruits, and/or nuts, combined with alcohol and a sweetener, usually sugar.

mortar: receptacle used in grinding substances.

peaberry: a rounded coffee bean as a result of only one bean developing in the coffee plant fruit instead of two.

pestle: club-shaped implement for pounding or grinding substances in a mortar.

petite: small.

piloncillo: unrefined sugar, usually molded into sticks or cones.

scald: to heat fluid(s) to near boiling point (do not let boil, especially milk).

sieve: cone-shaped strainer.

Index